Bismarck and the German Empire, 1871–1918

IN THE SAME SERIES

General Editors: Eric J. Evans and P.D. King

LANCASTER PAMPHLETS

Bismarck and the German Empire, 1871–1918

Lynn Abrams

London and New York

First published 1995
by Routledge
2 Park Square, Milton Park, Abingdon, Oxon, OX14 4RN

Simultaneously published in the USA and Canada
by Routledge
270 Madison Ave, New York NY 10016

Reprinted 1996

Transferred to Digital Printing 2005

Routledge is an International Thomson Publishing company

Typeset in Bembo by
Ponting–Green Publishing Services, Chesham, Bucks

British Library Cataloguing in Publication Data
A catalogue record for this book is available from the British Library

Library of Congress Cataloguing in Publication Data
Abrams, Lynn.
Bismarck and the German Empire, 1871–1918/
Lynn Abrams.
p. cm. – (Lancaster pamphlets)
Includes bibliographical references.
1. Bismarck, Otto, Fürst von, 1815–1898.
2. Statesmen–Germany–Biography.
3. Germany–Politics and government–1871–1918.
I. Title. II. Series.
DD218.A54 1994
943.08'092–dc.20 94–22013

ISBN 0–415–07781–8

Contents

vii

Foreword

Lancaster Pamphlets offer concise and up-to-date accounts of major historical topics, primarily for the help of students preparing for Advanced Level examinations, though they should also be of value to those pursuing introductory courses in universities and other institutions of higher education. Without being all-embracing, their aims are to bring some of the central themes or problems confronting students and teachers into sharper focus than the textbook writer can hope to do; to provide the reader with some of the results of recent research which the textbook may not embody; and to stimulate thought about the whole interpretation of the topic under discussion.

Acknowledgements

I would like to thank the series editors, Eric Evans and David King, for encouraging me to write this Pamphlet, for their very careful reading of the manuscript, and in particular their willingness to indulge the enthusiasms of a social historian. This Pamphlet is dedicated to my students at Lancaster who have endured, and I hope enjoyed, many hours of German social history. Their enthusiasm, good humour and refreshing insights continue to make imperial Germany a period worth persevering with.

Glossary and abbreviations

Bund Deutscher Frauenvereine (BDF)	Federation of German Women's Associations
Bund Deutscher Landwirte	Agrarian League
Bundesrat	Federal Council
Burgfriede	Civil truce
Grossdeutschland	Greater Germany
Honoratiorenpolitik	Politics of notables
Junker	Prussian landowner
Kaiser	Emperor
Kleindeutschland	Lesser Germany
Kulturkampf	Struggle of civilizations
Mittelstand	Lower middle classes
Reichsfeinde	Enemies of the Empire
Reichstag	Parliament
Sammlungspolitik	Policy of gathering together
Sonderweg	Special path
Sozialdemokratische Partei Deutschlands (SPD)	German Social Democratic Party
Unabhängige Sozialdemokratische Partei Deutschlands (USPD)	Independent German Social Democratic Party
Vormärz	Pre-March (pre-1848 revolution)
Zollverein	Customs Union

Chronological table of events

1806	Dissolution of Holy Roman Empire by Napoleon I
1814	Defeat of Napoleon
1815	Congress of Vienna
	Establishment of German Confederation
1834	Formation of Zollverein (Customs Union)
1848–9	Revolutions in the German lands and Habsburg Empire
1849	Defeat of liberals, conservative resurgence
1862	Bismarck becomes prime minister of Prussia
1864	Schleswig-Holstein crisis
1866	Austro-Prussian War, defeat of Austria at Königgrätz
1867	Establishment of North German Confederation
1870–1	Franco-Prussian War, defeat of France at Sedan
1871	Proclamation of German Empire
	Bismarck launches *Kulturkampf* (anti-Catholic legislation)
1873–9	Economic depression
1873	Three Emperors' Alliance (Prussia, Austria, Russia)
1875	Formation of Socialist Workers' Party (becomes Social Democratic Party)
1878	Anti-socialist laws

1879	Shift to protectionism
	Dual Alliance (Germany, Austria)
1881	Social insurance reforms announced
1882	Triple Alliance (Germany, Austria, Italy)
1884–6	Quest for overseas colonies
1887	Reinsurance Treaty (Germany, Russia)
1888	Accession of Wilhelm II
1890	Fall of Bismarck
	Lapse of anti-socialist laws
	Caprivi becomes chancellor
1891	Sunday working abolished
1892	Conservative Party adopts Tivoli Programme
1893	Founding of Pan-German League
1894	Resignation of Caprivi, Hohenlohe becomes chancellor
	Founding of Federation of German Women's Associations
1898	Founding of Navy League
1900	Bülow becomes chancellor
	Introduction of new Imperial Civil Code
1905	First Moroccan Crisis
1908	*Daily Telegraph* Affair
	Reich Law of Association
1909	Resignation of Bülow, Bethmann Hollweg becomes chancellor
1911	Second Moroccan Crisis
1912–13	Balkan wars
1914 (June)	Assassination of Archduke Franz Ferdinand
(July)	Germany offers Austria a 'blank cheque'
(August)	Germany declares war on Russia and France, invades Belgium
	Britain declares war on Germany
	Kaiser announces a civil truce (*Burgfriede*)
1916	Hindenburg and Ludendorff establish military dictatorship
1918 (October)	Military hands over power to civilian government, Prince Max von Baden becomes chancellor
(November)	Naval mutiny at Wilhelmshaven and Kiel
	Revolutionary unrest

		Abdication of Wilhelm II
		Scheidemann proclaims a republic
1919	(January)	Elections to National Assembly in Weimar
	(August)	Enactment of Weimar constitution

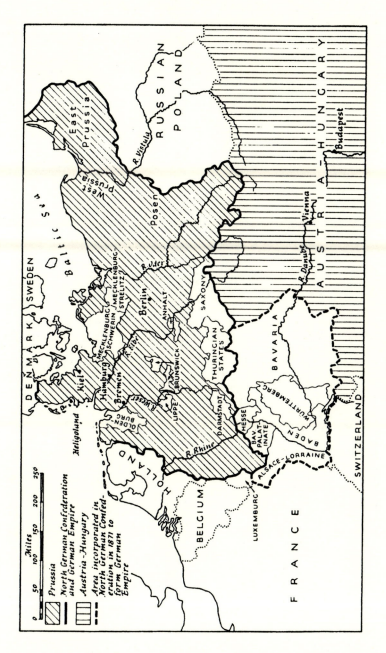

The unification of Germany 1867-71

1
Introduction

The second German Empire was proclaimed on 18 January 1871. More than a century on, having experienced authoritarianism, republicanism, Nazism and division after the Second World War, the two Germanies – the German Democratic Republic and the Federal Republic – united on 3 October 1990 following a peaceful revolution and the breaching of the Berlin Wall, a symbolic as well as a physical act. In contrast, in the nineteenth century the disparate German lands were unified by 'blood and iron', a political, diplomatic and military process culminating in Prussia's military defeat of Austria in 1866 at Königgrätz and her victory over France at Sedan in 1870. Prussia thus established her military but also her economic and political supremacy in a small German (*kleindeutsch*) state under the Prusso-German Kaiser, Wilhelm I, and the Prussian prime minister and German chancellor, Otto von Bismarck.

The new German state rapidly established itself as a leading world industrial and military power. From the mid-nineteenth century Germany experienced rapid industrialization accompanied by urbanization and social upheaval and yet this astonishing social and economic change occurred within a political and constitutional framework that has been labelled pseudo-constitutional, semi-absolutist. The new state, then, was something of a paradox. Germany failed to develop as a modern liberal democracy and thus, it is argued, diverged from the path

1

taken by the other major industrialized states, Britain and France, who had experienced their bourgeois revolutions in 1640 and 1789 respectively. In the words of one nineteenth-century historian, 'the proud citadel of the new German Empire was built in opposition to the spirit of the age'.[1]

The Empire lasted 47 years. In 1914 Germany embarked upon a disastrous war. Military defeat and exhaustion and disillusionment on the home front precipitated a revolution in 1918. The Kaiser abdicated and the old regime collapsed, to be replaced by the short-lived Weimar Republic. After merely fourteen years of a democratic republican regime, in 1933 Germany witnessed the reassertion of a far worse form of authoritarianism, when the National Socialists led by Adolf Hitler, came to power. They were to subject the German people to twelve years of totalitarian rule and another traumatic and costly war (a topic covered in another Lancaster Pamphlet).[2] Defeat was followed by occupation and division. In 1949 Germany was divided into the Communist East and democratic West. It was to be another 41 years before the German people were to be reunited.

Interpretations of the German Empire have been influenced by attempts to explain Germany's more recent troubled past, in particular the origins of the Third Reich. It has been suggested that the roots of Nazism are to be found in the Bismarckian and Wilhelmine era when an authoritarian political system was imposed upon a modernizing economy and society. The dominance of the traditional ruling elites and the apparent failure of the new middle classes to challenge this system supposedly explains Germany's divergence from the models of development taken by other western liberal democracies. So, it is argued, Germany traversed a special path, or *Sonderweg*. Instead of accommodating the new forces arising from industrialization she tried to deflect them. When this failed and the elites felt their position threatened they began to pursue an aggressive and expansionist foreign policy which culminated in the First World War.[3]

This view of Germany before 1918 as anachronistic, a dangerous combination of backward and modernizing forces, has dominated interpretations of modern German history in recent years. It has been reinforced by studies of the ways by which the ruling elites retained their power. It is alleged they resorted to

2

repressive and manipulative strategies to maintain their privileges and influence at the expense of the middle and lower classes. This scenario has been graphically described as 'a puppet-theatre, with Junkers and industrialists pulling the strings, and middle and lower classes dancing jerkily across the stage of history towards the final curtain of the Third Reich'.[4] However, this is a very simplistic picture. It tends to portray the German people as passive and easily manipulated and the elites as calculating and backward-looking. Historians who have shifted their gaze from party politics and national leaders and have examined the hidden areas of German society such as the everyday lives of the working classes, women, young people, Catholics and Jews, have shown that such repressive and manipulative strategies frequently failed. To return to our puppet theatre, the strings snapped and the puppets took on lives of their own.[5]

While the study of great statesmen and women has become rather unfashionable in recent years, historians of nineteenth century Germany cannot afford to ignore the role of Bismarck, the most commanding political figure in Germany for almost three decades. Bismarck has been lauded as a hero, a man of action, a truly great statesman, architect of German unification and Prussia's and Germany's great power status. Others have cast him in the role of villain, arch-manipulator or puppet master, and the primary cause of Germany's failure to embrace liberalism and democracy before 1918.[6] Neither of these polarized approaches does Bismarck justice although Bismarck's own attempts to justify his policies in his memoirs, published in the year of his death, 1898, are not to be relied upon either.

Bismarck once remarked after his fall from power: 'One cannot possibly make history, although one can always learn from it how one should lead the political life of a great people in accordance with their development and their historical destiny.' Yet few historians would agree entirely with this self-assessment. Bismarck was a key player in the making of Germany's history. At the same time, however, having set certain forces in motion – in short, having set Germany upon the path of economic modernization and social and political change – Bismarck was forced to 'cling to God's coat-tails as He marched through world history'.[7] Far from being the puppet-master, personally responsible for the tensions and difficulties of the Reich, he was instead the Sorcerer's Apprentice, a victim of forces which he was at least partially responsible for unleashing. Most historians would now agree that Bismarck bears considerable responsibility for the problems that beset Germany following unification. Both his style – he could be arrogant, ruthless and a bully at times – and his policies were not in tune with a Germany whose economic maturity was increasingly some way ahead of its political structures. His attempts to govern by exploiting a fragile equilibrium between old and new forces, between the monarchy and parliament, ultimately brought about his downfall. By 1890 he had become an anachronism; he no longer had anything to offer a Germany which had changed immeasurably since he had assumed office.

Wilhelm II, on the other hand, is generally credited with far less personal influence over the course of German history. Indeed, it has been suggested that after Bismarck's fall no-one effectively ruled in Berlin and one contemporary, his uncle Edward VII, described him as 'the most brilliant failure in history'. Wilhelm II certainly does not fall into the category of great statesman. While some historians have suggested that this erratic and complicated Kaiser and his circle of advisers did exert influence on foreign policy, the majority would agree that although Wilhelm II did possess considerable powers of appointment, he contributed little coherent policy to the decision-making process.[8]

In this Pamphlet I aim to provide an insight into the Germany of Bismarck and Wilhelm II between 1871 and 1918 by drawing on old and new interpretations. Chapter 2 analyses the political, economic and social structures of the new German state in 1871. The main theme of the chapter addresses the paradox of an authoritarian political system superimposed upon an advanced industrial economy and one of the most diverse social structures in Europe, and the problems this presented. Against this background I shall examine the consolidation of the Empire under Bismarck between 1871 and 1890 in Chapter 3. The strategies adopted by Bismarck and the ruling elites to maintain their position of power and influence will be assessed. Following the resignation of Bismarck in 1890 the Germany of Wilhelm II was characterized by confrontation as various interest groups began to mobilize on a collective basis to express their grievances, while at the same time, nationalist sentiment was mobilized

4

behind an increasingly aggressive foreign policy. Chapter 4, then, examines the diversity of Wilhelmine Germany and suggests that the Bismarckian nation state was a temporary or even an illusory entity. Chapter 5 describes the foreign policy conducted by the Kaiser and his chancellors which culminated disastrously in 1914. The experience of the First World War on the fighting and home fronts resulted in revolution in 1918–19 which ultimately brought about the downfall of the German Empire and the proclamation of the Weimar Republic.

2

The new German state

Before 1866 Germany as a political entity did not exist. After the dissolution of the Holy Roman Empire in 1806 and the defeat of Napoleon in 1814, a loose confederation consisting of 38 states was established. The rulers of the individual states possessed sovereignty over their territories and there was no German head of state or parliament, only the rather ineffective Federal Diet which met at Frankfurt. Prussia and Austria were the largest and most powerful members of the Confederation. During the period 1815 to 1848, known as the *Vormärz*, Prussia began to consolidate her economic strength aided by the formation of the German Customs Union (Zollverein) while Austria, which chose to remain outside this trading network, continued as the dominant political and cultural force within the Confederation. However, in economic terms, while Prussia was busy building railways and exploiting raw materials, Austria, under the arch-conservative Metternich remained a comparatively backward state.

The revolutions which swept through the German lands in 1848 and 1849 were sparked off by news of revolution in France, but they were fuelled by a combination of social and economic grievance and intellectual activity in the region. Nationalist sentiment was expressed by German liberals during the 1848 revolution. The new Frankfurt Parliament even reached an agreement on the future shape of Germany. It would be a united, federal state with a Kaiser and a parliament elected by universal manhood suffrage. However, national idealism was overtaken by regional practicalities and liberalism was defeated in 1849 by conservative rulers who were unwilling to cede power and a Prussian monarch who refused the crown of a united small Germany (*Kleindeutschland*).

Nationalism and unification

In 1848 there had been little evidence of popular or grass-roots nationalist sentiment and despite the emergence of nationalist associations and the spread of education, which promoted a greater sense of cultural and linguistic unity, the same was true in 1871 when the German lands were eventually unified. The German question was resolved not by speeches and majority verdicts favoured by the liberals, but by blood and iron as Bismarck had predicted in 1862.

In practice, unification can legitimately be seen as a form of Prussian expansionism. In 1864 Prussia flexed her military and diplomatic muscles over the Schleswig-Holstein question, defeating Denmark's attempt to integrate the two northern duchies and in the process stirring up nationalist passions in Prussia where nationalists had consistently staked a claim to the territories. The Gastein Convention agreed joint Austro-Prussian administration of Schleswig and Holstein but in the longer term Prussia became the dominant power in northern Germany. In the same year Prussia, now the most powerful state in the Confederation, won an economic victory over Austria by securing her continued exclusion from the Customs Union which facilitated free trade among its members. By this date Bismarck was set upon resolving the relationship between Prussia and Austria in Prussia's favour before the two states smothered one another in the competition for power and resources. Austria was finally defeated militarily at Königgrätz in 1866 in a war with Prussia ostensibly fought over Austria's refusal to renounce her independent policy interests in Holstein, but in reality it was Prussia's attempt to eliminate Austria from the Confederation. The frontiers of the North German Confederation, forming the core of what was to become the unified German state, were now established (see map).

7

Having achieved Prussian dominance, however, in 1869 Bismarck admitted that 'German unity is not at this moment a ripe fruit', while at the same time acknowledging that war was a necessary prerequisite for political unification. In 1870 Bismarck's exploitation of a crisis over the succession to the Spanish throne, resulted in just such a war. Bismarck's promotion of the Hohenzollern candidate for the vacancy in Spain enraged the French who interpreted Bismarck's move as a claim for Prussian dominance in Europe. Following the notorious Ems Telegram incident when Bismarck edited a dispatch reporting a conversation between the Kaiser and the French ambassador to exaggerate the Prussian rebuff of the French, public opinion in France was outraged prompting Napoleon III to declare war on Prussia. The support of the south German states for Prussia in this war guaranteed their eventual affiliation to the North German Confederation and thus their inclusion in a *Kleindeutschland* (lesser Germany). Following a Prussian victory over France at the Battle of Sedan the German Empire was proclaimed at Versailles on 18 January 1871.

The question of whether Bismarck planned German unification has been much debated by historians. Certainly Bismarck himself denied playing a determining role in the process. In 1869 he wrote: 'At least I am not so arrogant as to assume that the likes of us are able to *make* history. My task is to keep an eye on the currents of the latter and steer my ship in them as best I can.'[9] In fact Bismarck rejected a carefully planned policy since he believed there were too many unknown factors to complicate events. What seems certain is that he recognized that the political and economic ambitions of Prussia could only be realized at the expense of Austria, and moreover, the allegiance of the south German states to a greater Prussia could only be assured by a war fought in a common cause. The war against France, which aroused German nationalist sentiment, fulfilled this condition. Further, it is clear that unification was a means to an end. It allowed Bismarck to maintain political power by appealing to the national idea, particularly after 1866 when he believed the concept of nationalism and German unity possessed the potential to paper over loyalties of a different nature, for example, religious, dynastic or political. The unification of Germany, then, was the result of Bismarck's skilful diplomacy in promoting the interests of Prussia by harnessing national and

8

economic sentiment in favour of a *kleindeutsch* solution to the German question.

Bismarck's Germany did not assume the true identity of a nation state for several decades. Arguably it was not until 1914, when the German people came together as a nation to defend the fatherland, that a national identity emerged. In spite of being a geographical and political entity and not suffering the same degree of cultural and linguistic diversity of another new nation state, Italy, Germany remained regionally heterogeneous and the new constitution confirmed the federal nature of the new regime by permitting local rulers to retain control over the internal affairs of their states, including education, justice and local government. The imperial government held responsibility for defence, communications, currency and law codes, although a unified civil code for the Reich was not implemented until 1900. The south and east of the country retained its predominantly rural character while industrialization and urbanization gained a firm foothold in the north and west. Religious and ethnic differences overlaid this regional pattern. Around 60 per cent of the population was Protestant while Catholics, reduced to a minority after the exclusion of Austria, were to be found mainly in the south and the Rhineland. In addition there were minority Poles in Prussia's eastern provinces, minority Danes in Schleswig and French in Alsace-Lorraine. There were also ethnic and linguistic Germans left outside the borders of the new state. Germany's social structure was increasingly complex as new groups such as the industrial working class and the bourgeoisie grew in number and importance, while the old, consisting of the peasantry, artisans and landed aristocracy, remained numerically significant and influential.

Political structures

The new state was a Prussified Germany. Prussia was by far the largest state, stretching from the border with Russian Poland in the east to the river Rhine in the west. It was economically powerful, containing the major industrial centres of the Ruhr valley and the Silesian coalfields, as well as thousands of miles of railway track. Despite being the most advanced German state in economic terms, Prussia's political structure was amongst the most undemocratic of the German states. Prussian elites ran the state's bureaucracy, diplomatic service and armed forces and dominated the Prussian parliament which was elected by a three-class franchise heavily weighted in favour of property owners, thus ensuring the vast majority of propertyless citizens had little say in the running of the Prussian state. With Berlin as the centre of political power Prussia's presence was overwhelming. As Michael Hughes has noted, 'The German Empire . . . represented in military reality as well as in political effect the conquest of Germany by Prussia.' Prussia dominated the top two layers of the pyramidal political structure established by the new constitution. The king of Prussia automatically filled the post of German Kaiser; the Prussian prime minister became the German chancellor. Prussia dominated the administrative and legislative machinery of the Empire with its representatives outnumbering those of all the other states, duchies and principalities together in the lower chamber of the Bundesrat (Federal Council).

The German Empire was, in theory, a constitutional monarchy, yet in practice it was governed by a Prussian oligarchy. The Reichstag (parliament), whose 400 deputies were elected by universal manhood suffrage in a secret ballot, had little power, and often resembled a talking shop for political parties who were often little more than economic interest groups. All the elected deputies were empowered to do was scrutinize the budget and ratify legislation which could subsequently be vetoed by the Bundesrat. The Reichstag had limited independent power and could be dissolved by the Kaiser on the recommendation of the chancellor. Neither the government nor the chancellor was answerable to the Reichstag. Most political parties had rather limited social and economic bases and as the German social structure and population distribution altered the Reichstag became increasingly unrepresentative. The Conservatives and Free Conservatives on the right drew support mainly from landed interests but also from some industrialists. The two liberal parties, the National Liberals and the Progressives, represented the professional classes, the bulk of the industrialists and the wealthy middle classes. The emerging working class was represented by the socialist Social Democratic Party. The Catholic Centre Party, founded in 1870, was the most broad-based political grouping which drew support from across the Catholic constituency. Conservative on moral issues it had a progressive edge when it came to campaigning for social reform. The 1871 Reichstag was dominated by National Liberals with 125 seats out of 399, and with the support of the Progressives with 46 seats and the Free Conservatives with 37, they managed to secure a parliamentary majority until 1879.

The government was appointed by the Kaiser. The Kaiser's powers were extensive, incorporating control of foreign policy, command of the armed forces and the right to declare war as well as internal martial law. In addition he had the power to appoint and dismiss chancellors and to interpret the constitution. In theory, the chancellor was the Kaiser's agent but in practice this relationship was more ambiguous, as we shall see. Under Bismarck's chancellorship the regime has been described, perhaps not entirely accurately, as a plebiscitary dictatorship; after 1890 with Wilhelm II at the helm of a ship served by a series of chancellors – Caprivi, Hohenlohe, Bülow and Bethmann Hollweg – it has been termed an authoritarian polycracy, meaning dictatorship by a number of different groups. Throughout the life of the Empire, effective political power was held in the hands of a few belonging to the aristocratic elite. In a country undergoing fundamental economic and social change in the second half of the nineteenth century, the effective silencing of the vast majority of the population in the political process was potentially destabilizing. Political liberalism, the ideology of the western European middle classes, appeared to have been defeated in the 1848–49 revolution and it has been suggested that the bourgeoisie, the traditional standard-bearer of liberal values, was largely acquiescent in the political sphere. Having achieved economic power the industrial middle classes had no need to reform the political system, permitting Bismarck to continue with his reactionary politics. Karl Marx described the German Empire in 1875 as 'a military despotism cloaked in parliamentary forms'. Others have described the constitution as a fig-leaf hiding an authoritarian political system.

1871 did not mark the terminal date of the unification process but merely the start. Unification was largely a political process lacking any deep roots in the German culture. Consequently it took Bismarck another eight years to reshape the state and the parliamentary system and arguably another twelve years after that of attempts to manipulate nationalist sentiment in order

11

to integrate particularist interests into the nation state. The period 1871 to 1873, known as the *Gründerzeit* (foundation years) saw considerable economic growth stimulated by the currency reform in 1871, but the crash of 1873 signalled the onset of a severe economic recession. Until 1878 Bismarck relied on the support of the National Liberals to carry through his policies consisting of measures to facilitate free trade and economic growth. Steps were also taken to strengthen central government at the expense of the federal states which had retained considerable jurisdiction over areas such as education, health and policing.

However, Bismarck came under increasing pressure from landowners and industrialists, who were struggling to compete in a free market full of cheap foreign grain and imported manufactured goods, to introduce protective tariffs. In 1879 Bismarck broke free from his dependence on the National Liberals after the 1878 elections which established a Bismarck-friendly coalition consisting of Conservatives, Free Conservatives, the Catholic Centre Party and a section of the National Liberals who supported tariffs. This enabled Bismarck to introduce protectionism and therefore placate the agrarian and industrial interests. Thus began the shift away from liberalism, presaging a period of conservatism which continued throughout the 1880s, indeed 1878 saw the passing of a law to outlaw socialist activities. By 1879 it is not unreasonable to suggest that 'Bismarck's aims were first to interweave the interests of the various producing classes of Prussia and to satisfy them in the economic field, and secondly, to bind these classes to the monarchical state which was led by him'.[10]

The economy

In the mid-nineteenth century Germany's economy was still predominantly agrarian. In 1852 the majority of the labour force, around 55 per cent, worked on the land and in some areas, like Posen in the east, the figure was closer to 75 per cent. Between 1871 and 1914 the population of Germany increased from 41 million to almost 68 million, and by 1907 industry was the greatest employer, providing work for almost 42 per cent of the labour force. Yet, in 1910 more than half the population continued to live in communities of less than 5,000 people.

Compared with Britain, Germany was a late starter – her industrial revolution did not get under way until the 1850s – yet her transformation into a major industrial state was both rapid and remarkable. From 1857 economic growth significantly increased, stimulated by rises in investment, trade and labour productivity, and it was given an extra fillip by unification. A single system of weights and measures, a single currency, and common administrative procedures facilitated greater co-operation and increased trade throughout the German Empire. By the turn of the century Germany was challenging the first industrial nation, Britain, for economic dominance in Europe. But it is the combination of agrarian revolution, industrial take-off and political change that concerns us here, and in particular the reactions of traditional and new social classes to this economic revolution.

Many social commentators regarded the rural Germany of the early nineteenth century as a bulwark against revolution. They idealized agrarian society and praised its way of life centred upon the household economy, the church, and traditional practices. Urban society, on the other hand, was regarded as alienating and a breeding ground for irreligiosity and immorality. But rural society was not static and not at all idyllic.

Following the agrarian reforms removing feudal bonds in the late eighteenth century and legal reforms of the early nineteenth, the agrarian sector almost doubled its productivity between 1840 and 1880, stimulated by transport improvements, regional specialization and technical innovation. More land was brought under cultivation and more attention was paid to commercial crops such as potatoes and sugar-beet. The estate-owning aristocracy, particularly the Prussian Junkers east of the river Elbe, profited from the agrarian revolution. Until 1861 their land was exempt from taxation and these aristocrats retained their influence at the top levels of the bureaucracy, the military and the diplomatic service.

Rural society was profoundly altered by legal and technical advances. Farmers were obliged to produce goods for the market in order to survive which required the intensification of production and contact with outsiders. Goods were taken to market in nearby towns, and rural inhabitants for whom no local work was available would migrate to nearby villages and towns in search of work. Young women, in particular, were

13

often sent away to be household servants. The peasantry was not as backward and ignorant as many portrayed them. They maintained customs and superstitions only as long as they were deemed functional. Until the discovery and use of medical cures and remedies for example, rituals, such as exhuming and decapitating the body of the first victim of an epidemic to prevent further deaths, were common. With the introduction of artificial fertilizers and the spread of education, the vagaries of the weather, the causes of poor harvests and illnesses were better understood. In these circumstances, including the introduction of universal manhood suffrage, the politicization of the peasantry was inevitable. Peasant insurrection had contributed to the 1848 revolutions. By the 1890s peasant grievances were being articulated by pressure groups and political parties.

We should not be sanguine about the fortunes of the small farmers and peasants in this period. The peak of the landowners' power coincided with increasing uncertainty for wage-earning labourers who were affected by agricultural reorganization. As wages rose almost everywhere from around 1850, farmers began to invest in machinery enabling them to lay off farm workers and hire seasonal labourers when necessary. Subsistence farmers found survival increasingly difficult. The result was a widespread flight from the land. Between 1850 and 1870 around two million people left Germany for overseas, mainly for the United States, while the vast majority of landless labourers found work in the new industrial centres.

It was this internal migration that created Germany's industrial society. Districts which had been predominantly rural urbanized rapidly. Towns and cities grew at a phenomenal rate fuelled by migration from the countryside as opposed to a rising birth rate. For example, Bochum, a village in the Ruhr valley with a population of only 2,000 in 1800, grew so rapidly that by 1871 over 21,000 people had made the town their home, rising to over 65,000 by 1900. In cities the population explosion was even more marked. Hamburg's population grew from almost 265,000 in 1875 to close to one million in 1910, an increase of some 250 per cent. The number of cities with more than 10,000 inhabitants increased from 271 in 1875 to 576 in 1910.

Until the 1860s artisans outnumbered factory workers in most towns but German industrialization was founded on heavy industry's exploitation of raw materials – coal, iron and steel and engineering were the leading sectors – so that by 1882 workers in industry constituted almost 40 per cent of the workforce. The construction of railways acted as a catalyst for the development of other industries. The Ruhr valley was the powerhouse of German industrialization, where towns like Essen, Bochum, Dortmund and Duisburg, surrounded by pits and steelworks, attracted a huge labour force, but other regions such as Upper Silesia and the Saar coalfields and cities like Leipzig, Chemnitz, Hamburg and Düsseldorf, also contributed to the prolific growth rate. Gradually, large scale enterprises took precedence over small workshops. By 1907 around three-quarters of industrial workers were employed in enterprises with more than fifty employees.

Germany was privileged by her possession of abundant raw materials and the ability to exploit technology already tried and tested in Britain and Belgium. But the mode of financing German industry, the advantageous trading conditions and the expansion of the education system were equally important. Economic development was, to a large degree, financed by the state via the large banks. Prussia's membership of the Zollverein also contributed to the early years of growth as this system of tariff protection against foreign competition and maintenance of low internal tariffs stimulated trade in the long term. Prussia was also fortunate in possessing territories containing essential natural deposits and resources enabling her to establish early dominance over Austria. Finally, Germany placed great faith in the value of education. Compulsory elementary education had been introduced in Prussia in 1812, technical institutes were opened in the 1820s and a network of vocational schools was soon set up to train workers for industry.

After a period of almost continuous economic growth the German economy hit the buffers in 1873 with the onset of the Great Depression. Between 1878 and 1895 growth was more uneven until recovery between 1895 and 1913. This second wave of growth was aided by state intervention and the development of new sectors like chemicals and electronics. The Depression, which did not recede until 1879, had profound consequences. The period beginning in 1873 saw the organization of economic interest groups, nationalism of a rather chauvinistic nature, militarism and modern anti-semitism. The Depression caused the landed and industrial interests to mobilize behind the policy of

15

protective tariffs in order to retain their economic and political base. Thus, they succeeded in maintaining their power and the political status quo.

In the first two decades of the Empire, Germany had been transformed from a mainly agrarian to a predominantly industrial state. Yet this had been achieved under a political system which had not adapted to the demands of a modern industrial economy. When the economy faltered the reaction of the political system was to shore up the ruling elites by giving in to their demands for protection.

Society

Germany's transformation into a modern industrial economy was accompanied by major changes in her social structure. The most striking development was the rise of two new classes – the industrial bourgeoisie and the proletariat – but traditional social strata also found themselves forced to adapt to rapidly changing circumstances. The landowning aristocracy, far from dwindling in size and influence, consolidated and even strengthened its economic and political position with the help of the state. Once feudal ties had been dissolved, many landed aristocrats expanded their landholdings at the expense of peasant farmers. Some of them diversified and made fortunes from sugar-beet production and distillation of potato schnapps, forming a new agrarian entrepreneurial elite.

Another traditional group did less well. Shopkeepers, artisans and small businessmen, collectively known as the *Mittelstand* (lower middle classes), initially benefited from industrialization as the market for their products and services increased. Yet increased competition from larger concerns producing manufactured goods and the appearance of early department stores threatened to push this middle stratum down into the mass of the wage-earning proletariat, destroying their fragile independence. The *Mittelstand* regarded itself as the backbone of a stable society but its members found themselves squeezed between big capital and the industrial proletariat, unable to compete with the one but always in danger of falling into the latter.

The 1850s and 1860s witnessed the emergence of the industrial entrepreneur, the successful businessman who invested in and profited from the new industries. Men like Alfred Krupp represented the pinnacle of this industrial elite. Its members began to extend their influence in economic and cultural spheres, dominating local Chambers of Commerce and municipal councils. Some of them were almost like feudal landlords. Krupp, for instance, whose steelworks dominated the town of Essen, acted like the owner of a landed estate, playing the generous paternal employer by providing workers with carrots in the form of housing and recreational facilities while simultaneously wielding a stick against those who tried to join trade unions or the Social Democratic Party. Krupp and his family moved out of the smoky, dirty town to an ostentatious villa set in magnificent parkland, emulating the lifestyle of a landed aristocrat.

Yet, surprisingly, these businessmen generally failed to exert political influence on the national stage once the prime aim of protective tariffs had been achieved. From the end of the 1870s these industrialists gradually abandoned the ideal of liberal competition and shifted towards what has been termed organized capitalism, one of the manifestations being the formation of cartels – syndicates of businesses – in order to protect themselves from the uncertainties of the market. Neither, as we have seen, were many of these businessmen especially liberal-minded in their factory management strategies with factories not infrequently run on authoritarian lines.

The other new class created by industrialization was the industrial proletariat. This was an extremely heterogeneous labour force. Long-standing town dwellers mixed with migrants from the rural hinterland; native Germans rubbed shoulders with Polish migrants; Protestants and Catholics worked side by side down the mine or on the factory floor; skilled and unskilled, former peasants and artisans, men and women, provided the muscle-power behind Germany's industrial growth. Many took time to adapt to their new surroundings and maintained contact with their native villages, returning frequently and upholding traditions like absenting themselves from work on Monday (known as Saint Monday) after a weekend of drinking. Co-operation amongst workers was inhibited by residential segregation of particular groups, especially Poles and miners, and the high mobility rates of young male workers who moved from town to town, company to company, in search of higher wages. The new working class was fragmented. There was more to divide it than to unite it.

17

The living and working conditions of the vast majority of workers were extremely poor in these early years. Housing and public amenities had not kept up with the population influx so that single male workers were frequently housed in barracks or they became lodgers, sharing the same makeshift bed with a colleague on a different shift. Almost one-third of all working-class households in 1914 had one or more lodgers. Forty per cent of workers in Hamburg inhabited just one heated room in 1875. Towns were unhygienic; sanitation was often primitive. In Hamburg the failure to provide clean drinking water was responsible for the loss of around 9,000 lives in the 1892 cholera epidemic, the majority of victims coming from the lower classes. The infant mortality rate remained high at 210 deaths per 1,000 legitimate live births and did not fall significantly until after the turn of the century.

Working conditions were little better. In the 1870s workers typically laboured a twelve-hour day, six days a week and many endured a long journey to and from work too. Overtime could be demanded at short notice and it was not uncommon for miners to work one eight-hour shift immediately after another. Accident rates were high, especially in the mines and on construction sites. Although real wages had risen steadily before 1873 and workers were able to change jobs to take advantage of better conditions, during the Depression conditions worsened and workers began to suffer unemployment and falling real wages, at least until 1895. For many families meat was a luxury and potatoes and bread formed the staple food items. It was not until the 1890s and 1900s that workers capitalized on their collective experience and began to overcome their differences in order to challenge the power of the employers by joining trade unions and engaging in collective action in order to improve pay and working conditions.

Conclusions

By the time she was unified Germany was already on the road to becoming a major industrial power. Bismarck inherited a state that was already in the process of economic and social transformation. These changes were accelerated by political unification, but no attempt was made to adapt political structures to economic and social realities. By 1914 a dramatic transformation had altered the face of the new nation state so that the land-based population had fallen to around 40 per cent and over 20 per cent lived in cities of more than 100,000 inhabitants. And yet this state of Bismarck and Wilhelm II was ill-equipped to establish a comfortable relationship with the new social classes. Political power remained in the hands of the traditional conservative elite despite the transfer of economic power to the industrial bourgeoisie. In an attempt to consolidate this diverse and inherently unstable state Bismarck and his government embarked upon a series of ruling strategies which, instead of opening up the political system to represent those upon whose backs the state was being built, succeeded in cementing in place the structures of power more suited to a previous age.

3
Bismarck and consolidation 1871–90

Otto von Bismarck was appointed prime minister of Prussia in September 1862. He was born on All Fools Day in 1815, the son of a Prussian Junker and a mother from a successful family of civil servants. Bismarck was well educated in Berlin, a city he was said to hate, and after university in Göttingen he embarked upon a career as a civil servant. When he was still only 24 years old he resigned his post and returned home to the family estate in Pomerania but boredom soon found him engaging in Prussian politics. From 1851, in his position as Prussian representative to the Federal Diet of the Confederation in Frankfurt, he fought to maintain Prussian supremacy in the face of the Austrian challenge in the 1850s. In 1859 he was moved to a new diplomatic posting in St Petersburg but he continued to champion the cause of Prussia within the Confederation. Until 1860, as a diplomat Bismarck had been at the margins of power, but a constitutional crisis in Prussia, which saw open conflict between the sovereign and the parliament over the issue of the reorganization of the army, resulted in the recall of Bismarck from his posting in Paris to head a new cabinet. Between 1862 and 1866 Bismarck ruled Prussia unconstitutionally, ignoring the parliament, illegally raising the necessary finance by taxation and pushing through the army reforms. In his new position as prime minister of Prussia Bismarck sought to enhance the position of Prussia at every available opportunity. Just nine years later he had achieved his aim of securing Prussia's position within Germany and setting her on the path of economic success and political dominance.

It has been said of Bismarck that he protested too much and argued too much, ate too much and paraded too much, but it is undeniable that he was a skilful manipulator, a successful diplomat and something of a pragmatist. Upon his appointment as Prussian prime minister one liberal critic labelled him an adventurer and predicted his occupancy of office would be short. On domestic policy he was seen as a reactionary, an enemy of liberalism and not afraid of violating the constitution. Another critic predicted 'the rule of the sword at home' and 'war abroad'. There was some truth in this prediction as we have already seen. But after 1871, and particularly after 1878, as chancellor of the German Empire, his policies, particularly at home, appeared increasingly out of step with social and economic reality. Having unleashed new social forces, Bismarck's system could be described as crisis management in an attempt to contain the middle, but also the lower classes. In alliance with the ruling elites, it has been suggested he attempted to consolidate the new German state by means of repressive and manipulative ruling strategies. So-called 'enemies of the Reich' (*Reichsfeinde*) were suppressed, the German people were subjected to a regime of indoctrination, and attempts were made to manipulate nationalist sentiment in order to deflect political challenges and tie citizens to the benevolent state. As a consequence of the emasculation of opposition politics and grass-roots dissent, Germany under Bismarck and increasingly under Wilhelm II, developed into a society of competing interest groups, manipulated from above while tensions gathered beneath the surface. By means of what is known as a Bonapartist ruling strategy – meaning a combination of repression of opponents, plebiscitary elections, concessions to progressive, liberal demands and diversion of domestic pressures into foreign adventures – the German elites managed to resist challenges to their privileged position and indeed, maintained their power and influence until the 1918 revolution, having entered the First World War as a last-ditch attempt to deflect increasing social tensions and dislocations which threatened the political status quo. Such an interpretation of the period 1871 to 1890 places Bismarck centre stage as arch-villain, manipulator extraordinaire, master of *Realpolitik* (the pursuit of self-interest in the absence of ideology) and the architect of authoritarian rule. However, one could also interpret such strategies more charitably, as pragmatic attempts by Bismarck and the elites to deal with the forces unleashed by industrialization and unification using the only tools they had at their disposal.

Bismarckian ruling strategies

The heterogeneity of the German Empire was a thorn in Bismarck's side. Some of its constituent elements – namely Catholics, ethnic minorities, Jews and socialists – were identified as less than enthusiastic supporters of the nation state. Although these minorities never posed a serious threat to the state, Bismarck chose to label them *Reichsfeinde* and subjected them to policies ranging from discrimination to outright repression.

'Enemies' of the Reich

Catholics were the first group to be labelled and subjected to repressive policies. After 1866 Catholics were a minority in Germany. Constituting almost 40 per cent of the population they were concentrated in predominantly rural areas in the south-west and the Rhineland. Dubbed enemies of the Reich on account of their allegiance to Rome, and regarded by liberals as backward-looking and superstitious, a brake on Germany's development, they were seemingly ideal candidates for a discriminatory and coercive policy. In 1870 the first Vatican Council issued the doctrine of Papal Infallibility and in its wake, fearing the threat posed by clerical politics, Bismarck launched what is known as the *Kulturkampf*, literally a struggle of civilizations, but effectively a programme of discrimination against the Catholic Church. In 1871 the Reichstag passed the 'pulpit paragraph' which prevented the 'misuse of the pulpit for political purposes'. A series of Prussian measures followed which removed Catholic influence from the administration and inspection of schools. Then, in 1872–3 the Reichstag passed a series of far-reaching laws known as the May Laws or Falk Laws after their architect, the Prussian Minister of Culture. Adalbert Falk was motivated by his unshakeable belief in the complete separation of church and state. Hence, the Catholic section of the Prussian Ministry of Culture was abolished, Jesuits were expelled from German territory and the Catholic Church was subjected to considerable state regulation. The political voice of Catholics, the Centre Party, was also attacked on the grounds that the mere existence of a denominational party implied its opposition to the state although Bismarck's accusation that the Centre was a rallying focus for elements hostile to the Prussian state and the Empire perhaps provides greater insight into his motivation for attacking the party. In 1874 the articles of the Prussian constitution guaranteeing religious freedom were repealed, priests could be expelled if they violated the May Laws, the 1875 'bread-basket' law denied state subsidies to any priest who refused to sign a declaration in support of government legislation, and finally, in 1876, civil marriage was made compulsory.

The *Kulturkampf* was seemingly motivated by two issues. The nation Bismarck was trying to consolidate was founded upon Protestant Prussia. The Catholic Church was regarded as a dangerous independent authority, capable of mobilizing the Catholic population against the state and of stirring up nationalist passions amongst Polish Catholics on Germany's eastern border. Second, the *Kulturkampf* had a pragmatic political dimension. Bismarck was reliant upon the National Liberal Party for support in the Reichstag. Despite classic liberal principles such as freedom of the individual the liberals supported the *Kulturkampf* by arguing that the regressive influence of the Catholic Church had to be dismantled if the German people were to be emancipated as individuals. For liberals, Catholic schools, seminaries and even charities were symbols of closed minds and backwardness. Thus, the campaign can be interpreted as a means employed by Bismarck of securing National Liberal support for the government while simultaneously appeasing liberal demands for greater parliamentary democracy.

The *Kulturkampf* failed on both counts. In the short term Catholics were alienated still further from the German state. Ordinary lay Catholics demonstrated their hostility to the regime by refusing to celebrate national holidays like Sedan Day which usually took the form of patriotic displays of military pomp and ceremony. In strong Catholic areas like the Rhineland there were demonstrations involving thousands of people, public meetings

23

and attacks on state officials. So-called passive resistance was widespread: flying the papal flag, providing sanctuary to priests on the run. Most states lacked the administrative apparatus to enforce the repressive measures. In the longer term the *Kulturkampf* forced the Catholic community to look to itself for a sense of identity in a hostile Protestant state. An identifiable Catholic sub-culture emerged consisting of social groups, welfare organizations, trade unions, leisure associations and, of course, the Catholic Centre Party. Until 1890 the Centre retained the allegiance of around 80 per cent of Catholic voters and was the largest party in the Reichstag with around 100 seats. The rise of Centre Party strength subsequently forced Bismarck to abandon the Liberals. This also coincided with his abandonment of another tenet of liberal principle – free trade – and may be seen as the beginning of a more conservative era, signalled by liberal electoral decline.

By 1878 it was clear the anti-Catholic campaign had failed. In 1879 Falk resigned and the same year Bismarck switched to a protectionist policy with the support of the Catholic Centre Party. Indeed, the Centre seemed to replace the National Liberals as the party of government. Many of the anti-Catholic measures were repealed between 1879 and 1882 but the campaign had rendered serious long-term damage to relations between the state and the Catholic Church.

Poles, Danes, citizens of Alsace-Lorraine and Jews were also labelled *Reichsfeinde*. Poles constituted a significant minority in eastern Prussia and Bismarck systematically attempted to undermine them and Germanize them. In 1886 a Settlement Law encouraged the movement of German peasants into the eastern provinces, thus delimiting the power of the Polish aristocracy. Moreover, a series of language laws made German the official language. There were also thousands of Poles living in industrial centres who had been recruited by desperate mine-owners in a period of labour shortage. Despite the fact that they were contributing to Germany's economic growth they were victimized for their continued espousal of Polish nationalism and were forbidden to use the Polish language. Nevertheless, Poles continued to form their own clubs, publish Polish newspapers, worship as Polish Catholics and they even formed their own political party.

Just as Poles were regarded as enemies of the Empire on account of their allegiance to Polish nationalism and Catholicism, so inhabitants of Alsace-Lorraine, a territory ceded to Germany by France after the Franco-Prussian war, were suspected of harbouring dangerous sentiments for the French motherland. Here too, German was made the official language of instruction in 1873. Similarly, language laws and expulsions were used against the Danes of Schleswig-Holstein.

Jews, although formally emancipated throughout the German lands in the early nineteenth century, were intermittently subjected to anti-semitic attacks and discrimination. For instance, after the 1873 economic crash prominent Jews in finance and business became targets of resentment. Between 1873 and 1890 there were around 500 publications on the Jewish question expressing anti-semitic sentiment. In Berlin especially, where there was a well-established and sizeable Jewish community, Jews were targets of anti-semitic street gangs and their properties were damaged. The Jew was treated as a scapegoat for Germany's economic and spiritual ills. In the 1880s anti-semitism became more organized with the formation of anti-semitic political parties like the Christian-Social Party led by Adolf Stöcker who was elected to the Reichstag in 1881, and the German Social Reform Party, although single-issue parties were never very successful at the polls. Of course anti-semitism was never official government policy but these organizations received tacit support from the highest levels. Although several of those closest to Bismarck were Jews, his banker and doctor for instance, he never publicly opposed anti-semitism and indeed, on occasions he sanctioned blatant anti-semitic acts like the expulsion of 30,000 from eastern Prussia in 1885, of whom a third were Jewish. Bismarck's son Hubert was openly anti-semitic. Moreover, the Conservative Party became an outspoken adherent of anti-semitism. In 1892 it adopted the Tivoli Programme which officially incorporated anti-semitism into the Party programme, thereby tacitly sanctioning discriminatory policies against Jews.

It was the Social Democrats who bore the full brunt of Bismarck's repressive policy. Social Democracy had been slowly making progress amongst the industrial working class during the 1860s and 1870s. In 1875 a Socialist Workers' Party was formed from an amalgamation of Lassalle's Workers' Association and the Eisenach Party of August Bebel and Wilhelm Liebknecht. Standing for equality and democracy – values sadly lacking in Bismarck's Germany – the socialists were a potential threat to a system based on patronage and privilege. Although they secured a mere twelve seats in the 1877 Reichstag elections, at the grassroots level trade unionism was gaining strength. Membership of the socialist Free Trade Unions numbered 50,000 in 1877.

Bismarck was provided with the opportunity to clamp down on Social Democratic activity in 1878 following two attempts on the life of Wilhelm I. The first involved a plumber who fired two shots at the Kaiser's carriage, harming no-one. On the second occasion, however, Dr Karl Nobiling fired at the Kaiser and wounded him quite severely. Neither attempt had anything to do with the socialists but Bismarck had been looking for a chance to kill two birds with one stone: damage the Social Democrats and simultaneously weaken the Liberals. Bismarck undoubtedly wanted to vanquish the socialist presence in Germany but at the same time anti-socialist measures introduced in 1878, following the dissolution of the Reichstag and a swing to the right in elections, were designed to weaken liberal opposition.

In the event Bismarck partially succeeded in the second of his aims as some liberals supported him while others voted against the anti-socialist legislation thus splitting the largest party. The Anti-Socialist Law introduced in June 1878 and which remained in force for twelve years, had a similar effect on the labour movement as the *Kulturkampf* had on the Catholic community. The legislation did not outlaw the socialists altogether. The Socialist Workers' Party was permitted to fight elections and its deputies were allowed to take their seats in the Reichstag, but all other extra-parliamentary activity was strictly suppressed. Socialist agitators were arrested, imprisoned and could be expelled, socialist clubs were forced to dissolve (although many maintained an underground existence), socialist newspapers were banned and the Party was forbidden to collect financial contributions.

Despite constant harassment and vilification the Party gained in strength throughout the 1880s as the economic situation worsened and the industrial working class gained in confidence, partly aided by the re-emergence of trade unions. Workers continued to vote socialist in defiance so that by 1890 when the law was not renewed the Party, now renamed the Social Democratic Party of Germany (SPD) had 35 Reichstag deputies and almost 20 per cent of the popular vote. By 1914 it had more than one million members and was the largest parliamentary party with 110 deputies out of 397. Bismarck's policy had failed to weaken socialism; in fact the movement emerged from twelve years of repression stronger and more resolute.

Parliamentary representation did little to overcome the hostility and discrimination faced by ordinary socialist men and women in their everyday lives. In order to try to combat this, the SPD embarked upon the task of building a socialist subculture consisting of a cradle-to-grave network of subsidiary social clubs, sporting facilities, educational institutes and co-operative organizations. Many workers and their families were thus provided with a support network which lessened their feelings of alienation from a hostile state which had attempted to destroy their political representatives.

The Bismarckian strategy of repression of 'enemy' groups was arguably effective in the short term in that those affected were forced to retrench while Bismarck scored important political points and secured his political position. But Catholics, socialists and minority groups were not reconciled to the Bismarckian state and emerged from their repression stronger and better organized. However, they still had to struggle against a more pervasive and subtle attempt to consolidate and legitimate the new German state.

Ideological conformity

The policy of repression targeted specific 'enemy' groups. The imparting of a nationalist, monarchist and conservative ideology via the Protestant (or evangelical) Church, the education system and the army, was more insidious in everyday life. The values instilled by these institutions were designed to perpetuate the social structure and the hierarchy of power in German society.

Under the Holy Roman Empire each individual ruler was free to determine the official religion of the state. The state thus exerted considerable influence over the church and this situation continued until 1918 in Protestant areas of the German Empire. After 1871 the Kaiser was the head of the Protestant Church and in turn the church recognized the legitimacy of the state and used its influence via the pulpit and the classroom to ensure the compliance of the German people, instilling into them th of obedience, discipline and orderliness. Through the sermon and religious instruction the legitimacy of the Kaiser was reinforced. The Protestant Church undoubtedly preached allegiance to the German state and it upheld the conservative hierarchy, reinforcing the authoritarian role of the father within the family, the employer in the factory and the Kaiser in the nation. The relative absence of dissenting Protestant religious sects (in contrast with Britain) meant there was no alternative religious identity for those Protestants who rejected the covert alliance between church and state.

However, the Protestant Church was losing some of its authority owing to falling membership and declining church attendance. In urban areas the Protestant clergy soon became alienated from the labouring population on a day-to-day basis. Church building did not keep up with the population increase in working-class areas and church attendance on Sunday declined, especially amongst men who needed one day to recover from the exertions of the working week. Only 8 per cent of Hamburg Protestants took Communion in 1906–8 and while the church was still used for major life-cycle rituals – baptisms, marriages, burials – many workers reported they no longer believed in God. The German Protestant Church increasingly became the preserve of the bourgeoisie who publicly ascribed to the values of decency and hard work propounded by rather puritanical pastors. The Catholic Church, on the other hand, had traditionally appointed local priests and had maintained contact with the new generation of industrial workers by means of its social and welfare network. Secularization rates were consequently lower in Catholic areas.

One might have expected the Catholic church to have adopted a more confrontational stance towards the German state after the discrimination of the *Kulturkampf* but in many respects the Catholic Church and its subsidiary organizations may have helped to maintain the stability of the Empire by aiding the integration of Catholics into the state. On the whole Catholicism in Germany did not challenge the values propagated by the state even though it adopted a strong stance on the family and education. What has been called the Catholic milieu, including welfare and reform associations, women's and youth groups, and even trade unions, tended to provide Catholics with a home in a hostile Protestant state.

Despite rising secularization both churches continued to exert a powerful influence on German society, in the community via schools, hospitals and social clubs, in the workplace via the Christian trade unions, with 350,000 members by 1912, and in political life through the nominally Protestant National Liberals and the Catholic Centre Party, which lent an air of legitimacy to the status quo.

The German education system was relatively advanced compared with the rest of Europe. Most states had passed laws requiring attendance at elementary school at the beginning of the nineteenth century. In 1871 there were more than 33,000 primary schools (*Volksschulen*) in Prussia educating almost four million children. By 1911 these figures had increased to almost 39,000 and 6.5 million. As a consequence literacy rates were very high. By the end of the nineteenth century fewer than five Germans in one thousand were unable to read and write.

During the *Kulturkampf* religious influence over education was severely curtailed but Protestant values continued to have an impact on the formal and informal curriculum. With a formidable number of schools the education system was in a prime position in 1871 to take on the task of encouraging a sense of nationalism amongst Germans who were still divided by regional, community, ethnic and religious loyalties. Values such as loyalty to the monarchy, obedience to the state, discipline and hard work were instilled in pupils. Schools were instrumental in the so-called Germanization of non-Germans through the teaching of the German language, culture and history. History was given particular significance. 'Experience shows', wrote one primary school teacher, 'that the child must be acquainted with the history of the Fatherland and with the lives of men known to the *Volk*.' Schoolchildren regularly celebrated national victories and state occasions, participating in flag-waving and street processions, and nationalist and monarchist propaganda was disseminated through text books. Pupils read that their Kaiser was 'a man of true piety . . . with an unshakeable belief in God' and were encouraged to emulate him. At the same time, socialist ideas were also actively discouraged. Wilhelm II was especially keen to use the education system for this purpose and an education bill put forward in 1890 explicitly stated that its main purpose was to 'strengthen the state in its battle against the forces of revolution'.

29

The education system did not greatly promote social mobility. Rather, it functioned to keep every citizen in his or her place. Few were encouraged to continue their schooling at secondary level and only those who had the financial resources could afford to do so. Some did benefit from an advanced technical education which created a pool of skilled labour. The system as a whole perpetuated the power of the traditional elites. Only wealthy and well-connected young men progressed to grammar school and university. Fewer than one in a thousand university students in 1890 were sons of workers. Women were not admitted to the universities until the 1900s. Once admitted to higher education, students were rarely encouraged to adopt a critical perspective. They were trained to reproduce the views of the political and professional elite, and conformity amongst the student body was reinforced by student fraternities who perpetuated aristocratic codes of honour, including the duel. Therefore, the bourgeoisie, instead of challenging the existing system accommodated themselves to it, a process which has been termed the 'feudalization of the bourgeoisie'.

Military victory had sealed the unification of Germany and henceforward the military possessed considerable prestige, power and a good deal of popularity. The army was responsible to the Kaiser alone. Article 63 of the constitution stated that 'the Kaiser determines the peacetime strength, the structure and the distribution of the army'. Following military reorganization in 1883 the army strengthened its independence and neither the chancellor nor the Reichstag could limit its power.

It has often been said that imperial Germany was an excessively militarized society. The size of the army more than doubled from approximately 400,000 men in 1870 to 864,000 in 1913. Conscription ensured that all men had two to three years of experience of army life during which time they were imbued with a sense of national consciousness as well as discipline and ideological conformity. It was the unstated function of the army not merely to defend Germany against external aggressors but to preserve the internal status quo against alleged enemies like the socialists. To this end major efforts were made to prevent Social Democrats from infiltrating the ranks. Army recruits were not permitted to be members of the SPD and they were indoctrinated with patriotic notions.

There is little evidence to suggest these measures worked, but former members of the armed forces were recruited into the police force, lending that organization a distinctly militaristic character, and upon leaving the army many Germans joined a local ex-servicemen's association which enthusiastically participated in public ceremonial engineered by the state. Local shooting associations too regularly held festivals incorporating military-style ceremonies, much marching, wearing of uniforms and firing of cannon.

Along with the education system, the army, and particularly the Prussian officer corps, served to perpetuate the existing system. In 1860, 65 per cent of officers in the Prussian army were from aristocratic families. Although this proportion did decline to around 30 per cent by 1913, aristocrats were still overrepresented in the highest ranks. In fact the General Staff became even more aristocratic. Men from the middle class were accepted into the prestigious officer corps – a necessity when many sons of the aristocracy were following more lucrative careers in industry – but their background was subject to detailed scrutiny beforehand. Middle-class officers were not accepted as equals and in Prussia were derisively called 'Compromise Joes'. Once a man was accepted into the system of privilege and honour he was unlikely to challenge the power base of the military elite.

In view of the background of those recruited, it is not surprising that the officer corps was an excessively conservative institution. It jealously protected its code of honour which included the right to defend that honour in a duel, and consciously demarcated itself as a special caste. Under Wilhelm II this conservatism was manifested in the officer corp's determination to assert Germany's position in the world, thus supporting the aggressive and expansionist foreign policy of the Kaiser and his chancellors, coupled with a willingness to defend the state from the so-called enemy within.

Social reform and social imperialism

A combination of manipulation and diversion may be identified as the third strategy in the attempt to produce a collective loyalty to the German state. The ruling elite adopted the strategy of the carrot and the stick: an attempt to suppress the unsettling

31

and allegedly dangerous forces in German society and to indoc-
trinate all Germans with the ideology of the conservative elites
was combined with a counter-tactic of social reform and social
imperialism to head off the possibility of revolution and con-
vince the workers of the state's benevolence.

Bismarck is reported to have said, 'the citizen who has a
pension for his old age is much more content and easier to deal
with than one who has no prospect of any'. When Bismarck
introduced social reform legislation in the early 1880s, it was
not his sole intention genuinely to improve the working and
living conditions of the workers. Rather, he was additionally
concerned to maintain the stability of the system, and head off
the threat of unrest, by showing that the state could offer more
to the workers than the Social Democrats could. He was
implacably opposed to measures such as reducing the length of
the working day, restricting female and child labour and im-
posing a minimum wage since such reforms, although un-
deniably of benefit to the workers, would have alienated the
industrialists upon whom Bismarck relied for support. The
reforms implemented in the 1880s were of limited value, although hailed as progressive by other industrial nations.

The Kaiser announced a social insurance package in 1881.
What followed was sickness insurance in 1883, accident insurance a year later and old age and disability insurance in 1889.
Few derived much comfort in their old age from the pensions
legislation since payments were low and the qualificatory period
far too long. Similarly, the sickness and accident schemes were
riddled with drawbacks for the worker. A man injured in a
workplace accident was still likely to spend the rest of his life
in poverty. Only 10 per cent of claims were successful. It is
unlikely, then, that these reform measures would have pacified
the workforce. After Bismarck's fall in 1890 more progressive
reforms were introduced by chancellor Caprivi. Sunday working
was abolished in 1891, accident insurance provisions were
extended in 1900, in 1901 industrial tribunals were set up and
some funds were directed towards the provision of workers'
housing. Children were protected by employment legislation in
1903–5 and in 1911 all salaried employees were covered by an
insurance scheme.

State social reform did not pacify all workers. Often employers' welfare provision exceeded that of the state and the

SPD fought a tough battle to improve welfare benefits. Electoral support for the socialists continued to rise throughout the period. Employers, on the other hand, saw little benefit in state welfare legislation. They offered their own schemes which could be more directly targeted at specific workers. Company-owned workers' housing colonies, for instance, were one way of establishing a controlled and orderly environment and a stable workforce. The loyalty of entrepreneurs and industrialists was bought more successfully by the embarkation on foreign adventure and the quest for colonies.

Domestic politics and foreign policy are never mutually exclusive and in imperial Germany the two spheres were closely entwined. Germany's rapid ascent to become a major economic power threatened to throw the domestic situation off balance and the disruption of the hitherto smooth growth of the German economy prompted calls for a more aggressive foreign and trade policy. After the downturns in the economy of 1873 and 1882 a consensus emerged in favour of foreign trade and the acquisition of colonies as one answer to Germany's over-production. In addition to the potential economic advantages to be gained from a colonial policy, a second purpose may also have been in Bismarck's mind: to divert destabilizing energies at home into enthusiasm for foreign adventure and expansion.

Some regarded imperialism as a safety-valve, protecting Germany from a socialist revolution. We know that Bismarck harboured little enthusiasm for so-called formal colonies in contrast with his opposite numbers in Britain and France. 'Your map of Africa is very fine', he remarked to one colonial supporter, 'but my map of Africa is here in Europe.' Nevertheless, between 1884 and 1886 a number of informal colonies or protectorates were established in Africa: Cameroon, Togoland, South West Africa, East Africa, as well as one or two in the Pacific. Kiao-Chow in China was added later. For Bismarck an imperial policy was of most benefit in securing economic stability at home and thus pacifying the economic interest groups he relied upon. Already, by the early 1880s, other European powers were actively pursuing imperial policies, Britain and France in particular. Pressure groups within Germany, like the Colonial Union, founded in 1882 and the Society for German Colonization, which was formed two years later, made it appear there was considerable popular enthusiasm for overseas colonies. In fact this enthusiasm was limited to those who were most likely to profit from colonial acquisitions. Germany did not witness spontaneous outbursts of enthusiasm for colonies as occurred in Britain.

Under Bismarck, an imperial policy was pursued for three main reasons. It had an economic rationale, that is it was an attempt to maintain economic prosperity. It had a political and diplomatic rationale too in that it pacified the ruling elites at home while enabling Bismarck to demonstrate to other European powers that Germany was an imperial force to be reckoned with. Finally, and of least importance to Bismarck, an imperial policy was regarded as a social pacifier. Imperialist adventure would, it was hoped, stimulate nationalism and divert pressures away from liberal reform. This third policy, known as social imperialism, was followed more deliberately by Wilhelm II and Caprivi as tensions at home grew more dangerous after 1890. In 1897 Miquel, the Prussian Minister of Finance, explicitly stated that the maintenance of the status quo at home depended on 'diverting revolutionary elements towards imperialism, in order to turn the nation's gaze abroad and bring its sentiments . . . on to common ground'.

Foreign policy

In the realm of foreign policy Bismarck liked to portray himself as an honest broker. Having fought three wars in succession prior to unification, and having defeated both Austria and France militarily, Germany was now firmly established as a major player on the European and international stage. Bismarck claimed that Germany had reached saturation point, meaning she had no further demands and wished to consolidate her position. Thus, Bismarck embarked upon a system of complex European alliances in order to maintain the balance of power in Europe and secure Germany's position within this while placating those states which felt understandably nervous and resentful of the power of unified Germany, namely Austria-Hungary and France. At the same time, Bismarck's altogether more peaceful foreign policy after 1871 was designed to complement his domestic policy. An expansionist and aggressive foreign policy would have endangered the fragile equilibrium at home, yet Bismarck's moves to placate domestic interests, such as grain producers and industrialists, eventually set Germany on a collision course with its erstwhile friends in Europe. Thus, in foreign policy, as with imperial policy, domestic politics were never far from view.

Relations with the other major European powers had been influenced by the wars of unification. Austria, understandably, was nervous of her neighbour possessing far greater economic and military power. There were also still many in Austria who aspired to membership of the German state, but Bismarck gave them no encouragement and instead concentrated his efforts on winning Austria's friendship, hoping she would refrain from entering an anti-German coalition with another power. In 1872 the emperors of Germany and Austria inaugurated a special relationship between the two powers that was to culminate in the signing of the Dual Alliance in 1879. This alliance not only provided Germany with a degree of security in central Europe, it bolstered Bismarck's position at home by gaining the support of the Catholic Centre Party and others who had once hoped for a greater Germany incorporating Catholic, German-speaking Austria. In 1882 the Dual Alliance became the Triple Alliance with the inclusion of Italy. Under the terms of the alliance the signatories agreed to mutual assistance in the event of conflict between one of the members and another power, or in the event of an attack by France on Italy or Germany.

France had also suffered defeat at the hands of Prussia, but she had also relinquished territory, Alsace Lorraine, to the victor and ownership of this territory remained a thorn in the side of Franco-German relations up until the end of the First World War, when it was returned to France under the Treaty of Versailles. Diplomatic hostility between France and Germany was heightened by the so-called 'Is War in Sight?' crisis of April 1875. France had completely reorganized her army after the 1871 defeat and Germany now began to feel mildly threatened by a resurgence of France's military strength. The name of the crisis derived from the title of an article in a Berlin newspaper which raised fears of a French military threat. For Bismarck, who may have had a hand in the publication of the article and in any case was determined to see France isolated in Europe, the crisis backfired when the British and Russian governments made it clear they would not stand for the confrontational stance of

Germany against France. The crisis served to remind Bismarck of Germany's potential diplomatic and geographical isolation and in particular, he feared a Franco-Russian alliance. The failure to come to an agreement with France, despite attempts to ally with her against Britain in the colonial arena in the early 1880s, left open the possibility of a war on two fronts in the event of conflict. These fears spawned the Schlieffen plan, a strategy to defeat France quickly before turning to face Russia; a plan that was altered at the last minute and failed to work when it was put into practice in 1914.

Germany's relations with Russia were not immediately affected by Germany's new and powerful position at the centre of Europe and the Three Emperors' League (*Dreikaiserbund*) of 1873 between Germany, Austria and Russia, a rather vague agreement which did little more than bind the signatories to an association aimed at maintaining peace in Europe, appeared to affirm peaceable relations. But a nationalist flare-up in the Balkans in 1876, with the Russians seemingly backing the Balkan peoples against the Ottoman Turks, threatened to engulf Europe in a conflict. In 1877 Russia declared war on the Ottoman rulers, rapidly defeated them and became the dominant power in the Balkans. Throughout this crisis Germany had remained neutral and Bismarck established himself in the role of mediator, not wishing to embroil Germany in a Balkan conflict or destabilize relations with other European powers, particularly Russia and Britain. In the wake of this crisis, Bismarck enunciated his foreign policy objectives, his 'system', which envisaged 'an overall political situation in which all powers except France have need of us and are as far as possible kept from forming coalitions against us by their relations with one another'. Indeed, it was Bismarck's role in 1877–8 that established him in the eyes of Europe as a peacemaker rather than a troublemaker.

After 1879 domestic concerns increasingly began to have an impact on the conduct of foreign policy. Protective tariffs against imports of Russian grain, and a ban on trading in Russian securities on the Berlin stock exchange, imposed to placate both agrarian and industrial interests within Germany, were interpreted negatively in St Petersburg where the government was attempting to industrialize on the back of income from grain exports and foreign capital. Germany's hostile commercial policy, coupled with Bismarck's refusal to tie the fortunes of Germany to Russia following overtures from the Russian tsar, Alexander II, and the conclusion of the Dual Alliance in 1879, inexorably pushed Russia towards an accommodation with France. The revival of the Three Emperors' League in 1881 which, in addition to guaranteeing neutrality in the event of a conflict between one member and a fourth power, committed all three to respect of mutual interests in the Balkans, did little to cement Russo-German relations. As early as 1886, after Austria had intervened on behalf of Serbia against Russian interests in the Balkans, St Petersburg declared the Three Emperors' League dead. Strained Russo-German relations once more aided Bismarck at home when, in 1887, a majority of the Reichstag supported an army bill proposing an increase in military spending. That same year, amidst complex negotiations and alliances centred upon control of the Mediterranean and North Africa, Germany signed a secret treaty with Russia, known as the Reinsurance Treaty, which guaranteed German neutrality in the event of Russia protecting her interests in the Balkans, but this agreement was to be short-lived. The Reinsurance Treaty lapsed when the new German Kaiser refused to renew it in 1890.

Germany's relationship with Britain was less strained but better described as coexistence rather than co-operation, despite the close links between the respective royal families (Crown Prince Frederick's wife was the daughter of Queen Victoria). Britain, a parliamentary democracy, was always regarded as a political risk as an alliance partner. However, although in the 1880s the rival commercial and colonial interests of the two countries threatened to undermine even this peaceful coexistence, it was not until the post-Bismarckian era that the Anglo-German relationship took a turn for the worse with the expansion of the German battle fleet.

Bismarck certainly undertook European negotiations with some skill, but historians have debated whether the whole alliance system was constructed with any long-term aims in mind or whether it was simply a method of crisis management. There is some evidence from Bismarck himself that by the mid-1880s it was the latter. Each alliance, each treaty, gained Germany a breathing space. A war would have been disastrous for the German Empire and therefore Bismarck did everything he could to keep the peace in Europe. Perhaps it is this that partly explains the increasing failure of the alliance system to reconcile the competing interests of the European powers. It was constructed on an *ad hoc* basis with little attention paid to alternative centres of power outside Europe. As Lothar Gall remarks, Bismarck's foreign policy 'was bound up with a particular period of European history'.

While he has been criticized for keeping his diplomats in the dark – when Bismarck left office the Foreign Service was ill-prepared to step into the vacuum – the real legacy Bismarck left his successors in the realm of foreign policy was a system ill-suited to the new configuration of power in Europe determined by colonial expansion and economic interests in the world outside Europe.

Conclusions

The resort to a three-fold strategy in domestic policy which amounted to repression, indoctrination and manipulation by Bismarck and the ruling elites suggests that German unity was still fragile. Blood and iron had been used to forge the nation state but after 1871, when steady growth in the economy was punctuated by recession and Bismarck was no longer able to use the threat of war to rally support, rather different tactics had to be employed to maintain the power and influence of the elites against the tide of socialism. Once political and economic unification had been achieved, authoritarian and diversionary strategies were implemented to fend off the inevitable challenge of democratizing and modernizing forces. Parliament had been treated like an inconvenience and political parties were not accorded the status of representatives of legitimate interests to be taken into account. All this approach achieved, however, was a temporary lull. Problems were swept under the carpet and social tensions were left to smoulder. By 1890 it was clear that the Bismarckian approach to domestic policy was no longer practicable and his departure left his successors with a legacy of unresolved problems at home.

It is the failure of liberalism to gain a strong foothold in the political arena that lends weight to the view that Bismarckian Germany was governed in the interests of the elites. And at first sight it would seem Bismarck was successful in subduing liberal demands, reducing liberalism to political impotence. Little progress had been made towards a liberal democracy by the time of Bismarck's fall from power. Yet, before 1878 liberals were in the ascendancy. They welcomed unification and they supported the *Kulturkampf*. Free trade, a plank of liberal ideology, was an element of the Bismarckian system until 1879. Moreover, even after the setback of 1878–9 with the introduction of protectionism and the Anti-Socialist Law and the cessation of the *Kulturkampf*, coinciding with Bismarck's abandonment of the National Liberals, liberal values in the economic and civic spheres were far from impotent. Many elements of German social and economic life – a free press, an independent judiciary, a strong commitment to the concept of citizenship, the development of the free professions and cultural life and, of course, economic success – indicate that bourgeois liberal Germany was thriving outside the formal political sphere.[11] Such achievements were partially attributable to the existence of a strong state which guaranteed social stability.

In the foreign policy arena the Bismarckian legacy was equally problematic in the long term. His complex alliance system was unlikely to be sustained since it overlooked major tensions between the European powers and failed to take into account the changing face of European power relations. Almost immediately following Bismarck's resignation the decision to allow the Reinsurance Treaty to lapse brought about the collapse of this painstakingly crafted system. Nevertheless, at least until the early 1880s Bismarck's foreign policy did bolster his domestic position. He maintained the support of the agrarian and industrial interests by securing for them profitable markets in Europe and overseas, and by protecting them against cheaper imports. He achieved a *modus vivendi* with the supporters of a greater Germany by sustaining a friendly relationship with Austria. And he could claim to be indispensable by virtue of preserving peace more generally in Europe.

Bismarck did not succeed in smashing, subduing or integrating liberal and democratic impulses in German society. Rather, emancipatory and modernizing movements increasingly articulated their demands outside the arena of party politics. The picture of a passive, manipulated populace, repressed by authoritarian, discriminatory policies, indoctrinated

39

by nationalist rhetoric and with reformist energies satiated by social reform and social imperialism, is misleading as the level of conflict and confrontation which filled the vacuum left by Bismarck shows.

4
Confrontation and integration 1890–1914

Bismarck offered his resignation to Wilhelm II on 18 March 1890 after 28 years as first Prussian Prime Minister and then German chancellor. The young Kaiser had no hesitation in accepting. Indeed, he had twice requested Bismarck's resignation letter and was becoming impatient. Ever since the accession of Wilhelm II the Kaiser and chancellor had been boxing for positions. The precipitating factor in Bismarck's fall from office was his apparent intention to engineer a constitutional crisis over the renewal of anti-socialist legislation but the longer term cause was Bismarck's increasingly anachronistic policies and his inability to conceive of a future German state without himself at the helm.

Bismarck's political position was based upon his ability to present himself as the supreme protector of the status quo and foremost servant of the state. He had benefited from exploiting the fears of the traditional elites who believed their position was threatened by new social forces, namely the working class and its political mouthpiece, the Social Democrats. But this confrontational policy was beginning to pall and, along with the new Kaiser, people were beginning to question his tactics and demand compromise instead. Bismarck showed himself to be out of touch with the mood of the people and, more crucially, the mood of Wilhelm II who was keen to promote an image of himself as a sympathetic and reforming monarch. The 'red eat' was no longer regarded in such a menacing light and Bismarck's tactics were rather incongruous in a modernizing Germany. In May 1889 Bismarck once more chose confrontation during a nationwide miners' strike instead of searching for a settlement. It appears that Bismarck would have been happy for the strike to continue, to 'get out of hand', providing him with the justification for his next step: an extension of the Anti-Socialist Law for an unlimited period of time. Wilhelm failed to support Bismarck on the socialist laws and began to pursue a project of his own concerning welfare legislation. In January 1890 Wilhelm introduced his ideas for a programme of labour protection measures bringing him into conflict with the chancellor. Bismarck remained inflexible to the last, reportedly remarking that the social question was 'not to be solved with rose water but called for blood and iron'.

There is some evidence to suggest that in his desperation, particularly after the February 1890 election which produced a poor result for the ruling coalition of Conservatives, Free Conservatives and National Liberals and gains for the Social Democrats and the Centre, Bismarck was seriously considering measures to smash the Reichstag and guarantee his position once and for all. He underestimated the desire of the Kaiser to be his own man. Following another attempt to introduce an even more restrictive Anti-Socialist Bill for which he received minimal support, Bismarck received an upbraiding from Wilhelm including the criticism that he was a danger to the state. Bismarck resigned, no longer having the support of his Kaiser, the German people – who now knew the state would survive without him – and the majority of the Reichstag. Although many were sad to see him go, many others were relieved, a feeling expressed by the writer Theodor Fontane who wrote: 'It is fortunate that we are rid of him, and many, many questions will now be handled better, more honourably, more clearly than before.'[12] Unfortunately these hopes were not to be fulfilled.

Wilhelm II and the Bismarckian inheritance

While all historians would agree that Bismarck had a profound effect on German state and society, whether for good or ill, such unanimity cannot be found with respect to the impact of the new

Kaiser. While some stress Wilhelm's personal rule and place importance on understanding his complex and unpredictable personality, others regard his influence as marginal, depicting him as, at most, a meddlesome monarch. In the early years of his reign Wilhelm II was eager to be seen as a Kaiser with a social conscience, genuinely concerned to improve the lot of his subjects, but as his interest was distracted increasingly by foreign policy and the navy another facet of his personality came to the fore.

The circumstances in which Wilhelm acceded to the throne were rather sad. His grandfather, Wilhelm I, died in 1888 at the age of 91. The immediate successor was Wilhelm's father, the Crown Prince Frederick, but his life was cut short by cancer of the throat. Hence Wilhelm unexpectedly became Kaiser at the age of 30. Wilhelm had an unpredictable personality and in view of the power invested in his position – he had ultimate decision-making powers in foreign policy, controlled the army and could veto legislation – it is worthwhile considering some of his character traits.

Born to a German father and English mother, handicapped from birth with a withered arm and possibly possessing homosexual tendencies, Wilhelm exhibited serious problems in playing his exalted role. He loved dressing up in uniform, he played childish pranks and interpreted any setback as a personal insult. Foreign dignitaries were witnesses to extraordinary exhibitions of Wilhelm's odd sense of humour and offensive behaviour. On one such occasion during a visit to the Kaiser's ship by the King of Italy, Wilhelm remarked, 'Now watch how the little dwarf climbs up the gangway.' Practical jokes were regularly played on members of his own entourage. After dancing for the Kaiser dressed in a tutu, the head of the Military Cabinet died of a heart attack. Wilhelm was also easily influenced by a badly chosen circle of advisers. Witnesses to his behaviour expressed the view that he was insane. But it would be misleading to say that Wilhelm was at the hub of political life. Indeed, his influence may have been negligible; as one general noted in 1915, 'we haven't had a working head of state for the last twenty-five years'. Wilhelm was notorious for his indecisiveness, his meddlesome nature, and his interest in trivia as opposed to policy detail. He was no intellectual and was easily swayed. Many of his projects were defeated by the Reichstag and it seems that his personal influence on foreign policy and military planning was minimal. He was a loose cannon rather than a deliberate schemer.

Compared with Bismarckian Germany, which was a society coming to terms with unification and industrialization, Wilhelmine Germany was undoubtedly more mature and culturally diverse. The new social classes established themselves in Wilhelm's reign as conscious, active and persuasive entities. The bourgeoisie, the lower middle classes, the working class, peasantry and women began to find ways of expressing their demands within a political system still dominated by the traditional elites. Whilst the parliamentary system remained unreformed, interest groups began to mobilize often outside formal political structures. This mobilization suggests that the effectiveness of the anti-democratic structures and strategies pursued by Bismarck has been overstated.

Wilhelm's reign began on an optimistic note. The new chancellor, Caprivi, was keen to adopt a more conciliatory approach, and pursued a course of non-alignment with the parties in the Reichstag. The so-called 'New Course' incorporated welfare legislation to appease the left and tariff-reductions benefiting industrialists. Caprivi was perhaps rather naive in hoping for greater party co-operation in the national interest. Party politics was polarized with the Social Democrats gaining support, the Liberals divided and the Conservatives moving further to the right, embracing aggressive nationalism and anti-semitism. By 1892 Caprivi had alienated support from all sides – piecemeal social reforms and concessions to commercial interests pleased no-one – but his resignation came about following an attempt to reform the army, a parliamentary defeat and moves by others to manufacture a crisis by introducing another bill to combat 'revolutionary tendencies'. Caprivi did not support the bill but no longer had the will to continue serving a monarch he no longer respected. Thus he resigned instead of seeking to defeat the bill and the intrigues behind it.

The new government of the elderly Hohenlohe was ineffective. Under constant pressure from the Kaiser – who had by now abandoned any residual concern for the working classes – and others on the right to introduce new restrictions on the activities of the Social Democrats and trade unions, Hohenlohe shifted towards the right in an attempt to achieve a kind of Bismarckian anti-socialist consensus. This *Sammlungspolitik* as it was called, the gathering together of the agrarian and industrial elites, coincided with the beginning of a more aggressive foreign policy and expansion of the navy. Between 1900 and 1914 chancellors Bülow and Bethmann Hollweg were dogged by the instability of parliamentary politics and became increasingly reliant upon the unpredictable Kaiser as well as the army and bureaucracy to govern the country. Throughout the period 1890 to 1914 no effort was made to resolve the internal structural problems inherited from the Bismarckian system. In 1908 the so-called *Daily Telegraph* crisis had the potential to change Germany's constitutional condition but the opportunity was squandered by a weak and divided Reichstag. The London newspaper published an interview with Wilheilm II in which he made tactless remarks likely to damage German's relations with Britain and Russia. Chancellor Bülow, it emerged, had been shown the transcript in advance but had neglected to read it. When asked to explain himself, Bülow concealed his role in the affair and merely requested that the Kaiser take more care with his comments in future. Here had been a chance for the Reichstag to demand greater parliamentary power and greater responsibility of the chancellor to parliament at the expense of the diminution of royal privilege. Nothing, however, was done. Bethmann Hollweg, who replaced Bülow in 1909, was more sympathetic to limited political reform, but his feeble attempt to reform the three-class Prussian voting system had to be abandoned, and his failure to get the so-called *staatserhaltende* parties (parties of the status quo) to unite behind his policies meant he relied on extra-parliamentary forces to govern the country. From 1900 on, foreign policy was increasingly used as a substitute for domestic reform. The consequence of this was that the masses became progressively alienated from the formal political process. The result was a series of grass-roots challenges to elite dominance and counter-strategies by the elites to deflect these challenges.

Pressure groups and politics

It is important to remember that every man had a vote in imperial Germany, and that voters continued to regard Reichstag elections as meaningful events (between 1887 and 1912 voter turnout in national elections never fell below 70 per cent except in 1898). Indeed, it can be said that during the 1890s Germany entered an era of mass politics. There was mass mobilization of voters, modernization of party structures and electoral tactics and national issues increasingly dominated election campaigns. Yet, as we have seen, the Reichstag became increasingly impotent. Votes cast may have reflected the mood of the country but they did not affect the way the country was run. A space, therefore, existed for alternative interest groups, which operated outside party-politics. What has been called a 'political mass market' emerged in which the electorate was courted by demagogues, gradually replacing what was known as the 'politics of notables' (*Honoratiorenpolitik*).[13] Workers, women, peasants, shopkeepers, publicans, nationalists and anti-semites amongst others, began to bypass formal political channels and instead articulated their demands and grievances in public via pressure groups. Temperance campaigners, social-welfare reformers and pacifists existed alongside the more mainstream national organisations such as the feminist movement, the Agrarian League, Peasant Leagues and the labour movement.

The labour movement

Once the anti-socialist laws were allowed to lapse in 1890 the Social Democratic Party (SPD) went from strength to strength. It received more votes than any other party and by 1912 it was the largest party in the Reichstag with 110 seats. The socialist cultural and educational network expanded rapidly; almost every town had its Social Democratic choral society, sports club and cycling association. The very success of the SPD in this period suggests that the German working class was now stronger and less divided by religion, ethnicity and skill and that it was moving towards greater political maturity.

The twelve years of the anti-socialist laws had a notable impact upon the German labour movement and undoubtedly influenced its attitude and ideological position in the years before the First World War. During the outlawed years the movement put a great deal of effort into effective organization and parliamentary representation and it was not prepared to throw this away once the ban on extra-parliamentary activity was lifted. When the party published its manifesto in 1891 – the Erfurt Programme – the combination of this reformist, parliamentary stance with revolutionary ideology led to some fierce battles within the party, primarily between Karl Kautsky who had drafted the revolutionary sections of the programme, and Eduard Bernstein, the leading revisionist, who believed it was time to work within the state to achieve concrete improvements in the condition of the masses. This debate between the revolutionaries and the revisionists was to cause quite a rift in the party – a rift that was to become a chasm after the outbreak of war.

The SPD in this period was, by and large, a law-abiding parliamentary party. The party leadership was understandably afraid of the reimposition of repressive measures and was reluctant to undertake any action that would give the government the opportunity to justify even harsher measures against them. Indeed, even after 1890 socialists were still liable to be arbitrarily arrested and prosecuted for a variety of offences. The legal system continued to discriminate against the labour movement. This concentration on organization meant the party became increasingly bureaucratic, concerned with rules and procedure, and consequently it lost touch with many of the rank and file of the working class. Young workers in particular failed to identify with the ageing SPD leaders and the formation of the Social Democratic Youth Movement in 1904 was an attempt by the party to encourage young people to join while at the same time suppressing the militancy of young workers. In fact this policy failed. Young people deserted the SPD *en masse* after 1914. Women too found the SPD not wholly sympathetic to their demands. Although the SPD was the only party to support women's suffrage and equality of the sexes, in practice it was afraid of the Social Democratic Women's Movement and often adopted quite chauvinistic attitudes towards women members.

The SPD was increasingly incorporated into the Wilhelmine political system. Although the leadership continued to refuse to co-operate with other parties, thereby confining the SPD to a life of opposition, it participated in the political system by allowing its deputies to take their seats in the Reichstag and campaigning for reform. At the same time, the associational network of sports, social and educational clubs played its part in integrating the organized working class into Wilhelmine society. It was the aim of the Social Democrats to raise the class consciousness of the workers through cultural activities. In turn this would, it was hoped, increase the political awareness of the working class. Certainly large numbers of workers joined these organizations. By 1914 around 600,000 workers belonged to at least one socialist cultural club, be it a gymnastic club, a singing group or theatrical society. But this figure was a minority of the working class as a whole and most participants were skilled workers. Moreover, some of these clubs were not particularly socialist in outlook. Singing clubs often sang hymns and classical works as opposed to socialist anthems; sports clubs naturally engaged in competition even though they were encouraged to value co-operative efforts; and the books borrowed from workers' libraries were invariably the novels rather than works by Marx.

The labour movement consisted of more than simply the SPD. Trade union membership expanded rapidly after 1890 – by 1914 combined union membership numbered around 3.3 million – but this did not necessarily indicate a radicalization of the workforce. The unions were becoming more effective in bargaining with employers on behalf of workers and saw their role as extracting concessions from employers within the existing system rather than engaging in revolutionary activity. Trade union leaders were primarily concerned with long-term achievements and were frustrated by workers who engaged in spontaneous militant activity to achieve short-term gains. In many areas the unions were confronted with a workforce which had little in common other than the experience of work, and in order to overcome these divisions the unions stressed organization, discipline and a cautious approach so as not to alienate workers who might not have agreed with a militant line. The unions were pragmatic, they freed themselves from the SPD leadership and concentrated on practical issues: wages, hours, welfare provision and so on.

The organized labour movement in Wilhelmine Germany increasingly rejected confrontation with the ruling system in favour of accommodation to it. But the labour movement did not represent the entire working class and the activities of what has been called the *Lumpenproletariat* (rough or unorganized working class) suggest there was considerable confrontation between the lower classes and the state. Workers often defied the law or earned the disapproval of the SPD by engaging in activities that were seen as violent, criminal, deviant and immoral. They pilfered goods from the dockside, smuggled schnapps into factories when it was forbidden, and inflicted sabotage at the workplace. Parts of the Ruhr were described as resembling the Wild West and several towns in this industrial region experienced major incidences of labour unrest. Industrial unrest throughout Germany escalated in this period. Three general miners' strikes in 1889, 1905 and 1912 lasted up to a month – the 1889 national miners' strike involved 150,000 workers – and numerous small-scale disputes, generally over wages and hours, as well as lock-outs instigated by employers, disrupted German industry. In 1910 almost 700,000 workers came out in over 3,000 strikes; in 1914 over one million workers withdrew their labour. The vast majority of strikers were not members of the SPD; many did not belong to trade unions either and trade union leaders attempted to bring spontaneous strikes under control. Workers were also involved in more overtly political protest in this period. In Berlin there were violent riots in 1892 and 1910. In Hamburg, one of the states still to possess unequal suffrage laws, the 'Red Wednesday' riot in 1906 brought thousands of workers onto the streets on the day of the debate in the Citizens' Assembly on the reform of the suffrage laws. The SPD encouraged the city's workers to come out on strike and to attend public meetings in protest at the limited nature of the reform proposals. In the event it was estimated that up to 80,000 people heeded the SPD's call for disciplined protest but later in the day the protest turned into a full-scale riot – to the dismay of the SPD – involving the police hacking at the protesters with sabres. Observers of the riot made inappropriate allusions to the 1905 Russian Revolution. The Hamburg riots were not revolutionary and there were no revolutionary leaders, but the city's workers did demonstrate their profound dissatisfaction with a political system that disenfranchised them. There was a big gap between the skilled, respectable labour movement and the rough members of the *Lumpenproletariat* who felt the political system did not represent them and their needs.

Upon the outbreak of war in 1914 the SPD supported the government and voted in the Reichstag in favour of credits to finance the war, an act that some interpreted as a betrayal of revolutionary ideals. In view of the reformism of the parliamentary party throughout the Wilhelmine period, the SPD's support for the government in 1914 was not surprising particularly since the war was presented as a defensive war against Tsarist aggression. But the capitulation of the left brought to the surface many of the tensions which had been simmering since the debate between the reformists and the revolutionaries and it was not long before the socialists split, revealing considerable grassroots support for a more radical agenda. Those who opposed the war broke away from the SPD to form the Independent Social Democratic Party (USPD) in 1917. The final break came in December 1918 when another left-wing group, the Spartacists, formed the German Communist Party.

Between 1890 and 1914 the SPD and the trade unions gradually accommodated themselves to the Wilhelmine system, avoiding confrontation in favour of integration. The working-class rank and file on the other hand, only a minority of whom belonged to the organized labour movement, did confront the system on both an individual and a collective basis. The problems left by Bismarck were not resolved under Wilhelm II. The working class still did not have an effective voice, despite the fact that the SPD became the largest party in the parliament, and workers still felt their interests were in conflict with those of the state. This divergence of interests between a reformist labour movement and a radicalized working class culminated in the revolution of 1918–19 when the new parliamentary republic was protected by the SPD without pushing through any of the fundamental changes in the socio-economic structure of Germany demanded by the revolutionaries.

Women and politics

In Bismarckian Germany women were second-class citizens with no representation; they were subject to the oppression of the ruling classes and men in general. During the 1870s and 1880s women's position in German society began to change yet there was little possibility of real improvement until the 1890s.

Inequality between men and women was endemic in all spheres of German society. The law discriminated against women by treating them no better than children. Married women gave up all their rights and property upon marriage, and they had few rights regarding the care of their children. Women were not entitled to equal pay or equal education and, of course, they did not have the vote. Moreover, until 1908 and the enactment of a Reich Law of Association, women in Prussia were not permitted to engage in political activities, which meant they could not join a political party or a trade union, attend political meetings or form a political organization of their own.

Both middle- and working-class women experienced major changes in their lives during the final quarter of the nineteenth century. Women of the lower classes had always worked but in the industrial towns and cities women were forced to find employment outside the home – either in domestic service, in factory work or in any of a multitude of servicing jobs which were seen as an extension of women's domestic role, such as washing and sewing. Wages were inadequate. Employers often used the notion of a family wage to justify lower wages for women workers (men were regarded as breadwinners, women merely worked for 'pin-money') and generally women only received between 40 and 60 per cent of male wages in spite of the fact that few families could survive on the husband's wage alone. Employment for women was also unstable. Women could be hired and fired at will, they were most vulnerable to seasonal fluctuations in the trade cycle, and women living in towns dominated by heavy industries like mining and iron and steel, had difficulty in securing paid employment at all.

Few working-class women escaped the cycle of poverty. Single women could not survive independently while married women assumed the double burden of housewife and mother, and wage earner. Limited access to contraception before the First World War meant large families. On average, working-class couples had four to five children and some women spent their entire adult lives either pregnant or caring for young children. Not surprisingly the life-expectancy of working-class women, with their health weakened by hard work and frequent childbirth, was lower than that of men. In 1878 women were prohibited from returning to work within three weeks of giving birth but few were lucky enough to be able to afford even this luxury.

The lives of middle-class women changed too, but in different ways. The daughters and wives of the bourgeoisie were undoubtedly more privileged than their working-class sisters but they were trapped by a middle-class domestic ideology which confined them to the home, the so-called private sphere.

Few middle-class households were wealthy enough to be able to afford more than one servant which meant that the lady of the house had to undertake a great deal of work in order to maintain the appearance of a respectable bourgeois lifestyle. This was a period of greater opportunities in the world of paid work but these opportunities were barred to all but a few women. Women's education was inadequate. Working-class women received the basics – reading, writing and needlework – while women of the middle class were taught cultural accomplishments but little else. There were few secondary schools for women until the eve of the war, women were not permitted to take the high school examination, the *Abitur*, until 1895; and it was not until the 1900s that women could attend university. Clearly then, women's horizons were limited by a discriminatory system. Working-class women were forced to take poorly paid, monotonous jobs while middle-class women were lucky if they became primary-school teachers. The professions – law, medicine, higher education – were out of reach for all but the very persistent.

Most political parties paid scant attention to the position of women. Only the Social Democrats supported women's demands for equal rights and even they failed to back up their statements with action. So women who wished to see changes began to organize independently of political parties. The first women's organization, the General German Women's Association founded by Louise Otto-Peters in 1865, had been primarily concerned with equal education and access to the professions, but had achieved little by the end of the Bismarckian era. In the 1880s and 1890s two organizations began to campaign for women's rights: the bourgeois women's movement which, as the Federation of German Women's Associations (Bund Deutscher Frauenvereine, BDF) had around 12,000 members in 1894, and the Socialist Women's Movement led by Clara Zetkin and later Luise Zietz. The relaxation of the political atmosphere following Bismarck's fall benefited the women's movement but it also brought the women's question to public prominence, revealing another hornet's nest for the Wilhelmine regime to deal with.

As long as the women's movement concentrated on issues like education and equal pay the government lost little sleep over what it called the woman question, but around the turn of the century the movement became more radical, especially when women realized that the new Civil Code for unified Germany, due to be implemented in 1900, would do little to improve women's legal position and in some respects made things worse; for instance, the divorce law was made more restrictive. Women activists received little support from the men in the Reichstag, prompting the view that if women were to play a full part in decision-making they had to be given the vote. The BDF under a new leader, Marie Stritt, began to campaign for women's suffrage as well as opposing state-regulated prostitution and supporting the legalization of abortion.

This brief radical phase came to a halt in 1908 when women were given the right to engage in politics following the Law of Association. As a consequence thousands of women who had been reluctant to join the women's movement beforehand flooded into the BDF, and a majority of these women were conservative in outlook. For example, 8,000 members of the German Evangelical Women's League joined the BDF in 1908. Marie Stritt was replaced as leader by the more moderate Gertrud Bäumer, and henceforward the BDF reverted to extolling the virtues of motherhood and women's special qualities.

At the same time the Social Democratic women's organization was recruiting working-class women and campaigning for improvements in women's working conditions. Under the inspiration of Clara Zetkin the movement fought against restrictions on women's employment and encouraged women to join the SPD since emancipation could only be achieved, according to the socialists, after a socialist revolution. On International Women's Day, 8 March, thousands of women regularly demonstrated for the vote. By 1914 almost 175,000 women were affiliated to the SPD. It supported women's suffrage and involved itself in female and child welfare. The socialist women's organization refused to co-operate with the BDF even when they had much in common, since although the BDF claimed it was campaigning on behalf of all women the socialist women maintained that women's emancipation would only come about with the emancipation of the entire working class. Bourgeois women in the BDF were seen by some socialist women as just as exploitative of working-class women as men were.

Under Bismarck the women's movement had been immature and shackled by restrictions on women's ability to organize collectively. After 1890 feminists adopted a more confrontational stance with the regime. They raised the woman question to an issue of national importance and found a voice outside the confines of party politics. After 1908, however, despite the fact that little of substance had been achieved, many women found some accommodation with the regime and adopted a more pragmatic stance. By the outbreak of war there had been some limited improvement in the position of German women. The length of the working day had been reduced, there were some educational improvements, and married women now had full legal status. But women had to wait for a new regime after the war and revolution for full constitutional equality and the vote.

Peasants and peasant leagues

During the 1890s politics infiltrated the countryside as peasants and landlords mobilized to protect their interests. Peasants and farmers had been affected by industrialization and competition from overseas and the Junker-dominated Agrarian League (Bund der Landwirte) was formed in 1893 as a pressure group to campaign for protection for domestic agricultural produce. The Agrarian League masqueraded as an independent force but it was clearly aiming to attract peasant votes away from the SPD, who had already made inroads in some rural areas. The League soon became a dominant force within the Conservative Party. The Agrarian League was most successful in attracting peasant support in the Protestant north and it achieved some success in mobilizing votes on the protection issue in the Reichstag elections of 1898 and 1903. In the south, however, and especially in Catholic Bavaria, the peasantry tended to reject the old elites as their representatives. Instead, during the 1890s the peasantry mobilized from below, forming radical organizations called Peasant Leagues. These successfully articulated the fears and needs of the rural electorate and in some parts of Germany, notably Bavaria, they gained considerable electoral support at the expense of the Catholic Centre Party.

The Peasant Leagues reacted to the economic pressure on peasants who had been suffering for years from high land prices, high interest rates and a decline in income after 1890 which meant there was little available capital to plough back into improvements. Southern Germany was also affected by a severe drought in 1893. In order to remedy this situation the Peasant Leagues called for a reduction in the financial burdens on peasants combined with a reduction in state expenditure, especially the vast amounts spent on the military. This final demand brought the Leagues into conflict with the Agrarian League which supported increases in military expenditure. Central to the Peasant Leagues' stance was the attack on authority and state bureaucracy.

The peasantry in Wilhelmine Germany had matured as a result of economic pressure and greater political mobilization in the countryside. The Leagues succeeded in arousing considerable concern within the government who likened them to the Social Democrats, radicals who threatened political stability. They also inspired the Centre Party to start actively mobilizing peasants and listening more carefully to their grievances instead of merely relying on them for electoral support. The Centre had relied quite heavily on rural voters but it was losing out to the more radical programme of the Peasant Leagues. In the 1890s Catholic Peasant Associations began to emerge, adopting a similar programme to the Leagues.

The existence of the Leagues and the Catholic Peasant Associations indicates another group in Wilhelmine Germany which challenged the existing system with radical politics and which succeeded in mobilizing a sector of the population behind a radical agenda. The Agrarian League was successful in Protestant areas, adopting a programme of economic conservatism and thinly-veiled anti-semitism to attract small farmers and peasants but in Catholic regions grass-roots peasant organizations were more representative of peasant discontent.

Nationalist pressure groups

Pressure-group politics and agitation was not confined to the left. The 1890s and 1900s saw the formation of a number of nationalist pressure groups which soon boasted extensive support. But these organizations were not always challenging the status quo. Rather, they served as a useful tool of the ruling classes for the purpose of mobilizing popular support in favour of government policy, especially an aggressive foreign and colonial policy and the development of a large navy. All these policies furthered the interests of the dominant classes, especially representatives of heavy industry whose success depended on government contracts for arms and military hardware and the development of overseas markets.

The most prominent and largest of these organizations were the German Colonial Society (founded in 1887), the Pan-German League (1891), the Navy League (1898) and the Army League (1912). These pressure groups did manage to mobilize a significant sector of the population. At its peak in 1902 the Pan-German League, which campaigned on a programme of *völkisch* (radical conservative) nationalism and an aggressive warship construction programme, had more than 22,000 members. The Navy League, probably the most important amongst nationalist pressure groups, which explicitly supported Admiral von Tirpitz's battle fleet programme, boasted around 200,000 members after just eighteen months. The Navy League was founded by Krupp, the steel magnate, and was primarily financed by heavy industry. Krupp was in an ideal position to benefit from the battleship-building programme since his company was the only manufacturer of the armour-plating used for warships. But other industrialists were also happy to support a programme which not only saved the jobs of those in the shipbuilding industry but helped to stabilize the economy as a whole by stimulating production.

These pressure groups occupied the middle ground in German politics between the government and the political parties. They ran effective propaganda machines and foisted themselves onto the political stage, attracting attention for their clear aims and objectives, in contrast with the wheeling and dealing of party politics under Wilhelm II. In fact groups like these did not, in the main, try to directly influence election campaigns, neither did they try to challenge the established parties. They simply helped to define the electoral agenda. The most notable exception was the so-called Hottentot election in 1907, when the radical nationalist organizations were used to amass support for the government against the 'enemies of the Reich', in this case the socialists and the Centre. However, it is doubtful whether these organizations succeeded in mobilizing widespread popular opinion behind government policy. Right-wing pressure groups inevitably drew support from a particular sector of the population, namely urban, middle-class men. Amongst the office-holders of the Pan-German League, for instance, merely 1 per cent had a working-class background and only 2 per cent came from the nobility. While the middle class may also have seen the economic benefits to be gained from a stimulation of trade and protection, they were more concerned with the threat of the socialists on the one hand and the status of Germany as a world power on the other. These two motives for supporting nationalist groups were closely connected. It was thought that the patriotism engendered by colonial expansion and naval supremacy would act as a palliative against the Social Democrats. In short, these pressure groups aimed to stabilize the political system by diverting the energies of destabilizing elements while at the same time gathering together conservative forces behind the government, so-called *Sammlungspolitik*. They did succeed to some extent in radicalizing right-wing politics but they failed to make any deep-seated impression on the mass of the German population. Indeed, the SPD made political capital from the demands for increased expenditure by these groups. Working people began to question the proportion of their taxes spent on the armed forces in contrast with the proportion spent on welfare.

Anti-semitic groups should also be mentioned here. The first anti-semitic pressure group (deceptively known as *Reformvereine* or Reform Associations) was founded in 1879, after the historian Heinrich von Treitschke wrote, 'the Jews are our national misfortune'. By the Wilhelmine period there were *Reformvereine* in every German town, but in contrast with other right-wing pressure groups the anti-semites did contest regional and national elections as independent candidates. They achieved a breakthrough in the Reichstag elections of 1893, in some regions receiving up to 15 per cent of the popular vote, but anti-semites never transcended their status as a focus for protest against the parties of the right, especially the Conservatives, and political anti-semitism in general failed to establish itself as a permanent feature of the German political scene.

Conclusions

Wilhelmine Germany was somewhat less stable than the Bismarckian regime. Bismarck had succeeded, to some extent, in consolidating the state by the suppression of potentially destabilizing elements and manipulation of the political system.

But Bismarck achieved short-term stability at the expense of long-term solutions. He only temporarily succeeded in consolidating the German state because potential opposition had its attention elsewhere: on social problems arising from industrialization, on dealing with political repression, on establishing successful industrial enterprises. After 1890 the growth of mass politicization and the more sophisticated articulation of grievances via pressure groups as well as political parties, threatened to destabilize the fragile status quo painstakingly constructed by the ruling elites. The politics of notables no longer satisfied a more sophisticated electorate. Workers, women and peasants challenged the elites by casting their votes for alternative parties, forming pressure groups or by taking direct action: strikes, marches and public demonstrations and disturbances were not uncommon in this period. The elite response was recourse to radical nationalism which lobbied in favour of an acquisitive imperialism, aggressive foreign policy and military build-up. Wilhelmine Germany erected a commanding façade of monarchical splendour and military power but this concealed political disintegration and heightened social tension. The outbreak of war in 1914 only achieved a temporary national consensus.

5

War and revolution 1914–18

The road to war

German foreign policy assumed a more aggressive and expansionist character under Wilhelm II. From the late 1890s, under the governments of Hohenlohe and Bülow, foreign and imperial policy assumed greater importance on the domestic scene. As we have seen, there had been attempts to whip up nationalist enthusiasm at home in support of the expansion of the German fleet and a more assertive foreign policy.

The Kaiser had refused to renew the Reinsurance Treaty with Russia in 1890, having been badly advised by Caprivi and the Foreign Ministry that it offered Germany few advantages, and this pushed the Russians towards an alliance with France. Britain, whose attempts to draw closer to Germany had been frustrated, began to seek an understanding with the French, and an Anglo-French *entente* was signed in 1904. Thus, in the space of five years the Bismarckian alliance system had been dismantled and Germany found herself isolated, surrounded by potentially hostile powers, exposed to a potential war on two fronts, with only Austria-Hungary as a friend. Wilhelm II's influence over the direction and character of some aspects of German foreign policy, particularly the battleship programme, was evident. The Kaiser was strongly influenced by Admiral von Tirpitz, who nurtured in him a love of the navy. Tirpitz had already contributed to the alienation of Russia by seizing Kiao-Chow in 1897, a territory regarded by Russia as within her sphere of influence in northern China. At the head of the Admiralty Tirpitz embarked upon a campaign which was to alienate Britain too. With Wilhelm II's support Tirpitz began to transform the navy in order to rival Britain's naval power. This campaign had the side-effect of enabling chancellor Bülow to rally behind the government all those who supported the policy and who were afraid of the socialists. These included industrialists, chambers of commerce and the finance industry, as well as the Pan-German League, the Colonial Union and, after 1898, the Navy League. In 1898 Tirpitz's Naval Bill which provided for an increase in the number of battleships to nineteen, and a Supplementary Bill two years later which doubled that number, proceeded successfully through the Reichstag. It is not surprising that this naval expansion undermined relations between Britain and Germany.

Wilhelm II was probably more belligerent than his final chancellor Bethmann Hollweg, who did try to adopt a calmer and more conciliatory foreign policy, but by this time it was impossible for him to achieve a parliamentary majority in support of his policies and the country was being governed by the military with the support of the Kaiser. Bethmann Hollweg tried to reach agreement with Britain over the escalating naval race in order to bring the seemingly endless and futile competition to an end, but his internal position was weak and external pressures exposed this. During the second Moroccan Crisis of 1911 Germany's isolation in Europe was highlighted and the military and patriotic interests within Germany lost confidence in the chancellor's ability to deal with the international situation. When troubles flared in the Balkans in 1912, threatening to embroil all the major European powers in a war, Bethmann Hollweg lost his nerve, hoping at best for a settlement and at worst a limited war. This is not the place to rehearse the events leading up to the First World War; another Lancaster Pamphlet deals with this in detail.[14] Suffice it to say, when Germany agreed to support Austrian retaliatory actions against Serbia, giving the famous 'blank cheque' in response to the assassination of Archduke Franz Ferdinand, Austrian heir to the throne, in Sarajevo on 28 June 1914, neither Bethmann Hollweg nor Wilhelm II, nor even the military fully appreciated the consequences of their actions. None expected the ensuing war to be so long or to be so destructive.

Germany's responsibility for the outbreak of war has been debated at length. In 1961 Fritz Fischer controversially argued that Germany not only bore full responsibility for the war but furthermore, that under Wilhelm II she had planned a war in order to achieve great-power status. In the 1970s Hans-Ulrich Wehler developed a parallel argument to the Fischer thesis. Wehler emphasized the primacy of domestic policy in the development of foreign policy and proposed that the anachronistic character of the Second Empire was to blame for the descent into war. By 1914 war was the only and final means by which the ruling elites could seek to maintain their power against the threat of new social forces, an 'escape forwards'.[15] Both of these views have much to recommend them. However, when we examine Germany's experience of war on the home and the fighting fronts it becomes clear that even if Germany was responsible for the outbreak of war, she had not prepared for the conditions of 'total war' that were to characterize the years 1914 to 1918.

The experience of war

The outbreak of war in August 1914 was greeted in Germany, as elsewhere in Europe, with considerable jubilation and patriotic enthusiasm. Germans were convinced they were fighting a defensive war against Russia, a war they had been provoked into entering once the Russians had mobilized against Austria in defence of Serbia. All the political parties rallied to the war effort, including the SPD. With the words, 'I no longer recognize parties; I only recognize Germans', Wilhelm II announced a civil truce (*Burgfriede*). Many on the right believed the war was an ideal solution to the conflicts and problems which had beset Wilhelm's reign. The threat of an attack from Tsarist Russia permitted the majority on the political left to abandon their blanket opposition to imperialist wars although the SPD and the trade unions expected to be rewarded for their support with the reform of the political system.

The soldiers who marched to war in August 1914 were acting in accordance with the now notorious Schlieffen Plan. This plan envisaged the invasion of France via neutral Belgium in order to defeat France quickly before turning to meet the Russians, thus avoiding a war on two fronts. The plan was not a success. Belgium put up quite a fight, which delayed German entry into France and allowed the British time to marshal troops to defend her ally. Thenceforth, German, French and British troops became bogged down in trench warfare which claimed the lives of tens of thousands of men for nothing as successive battles ended in stalemate. Not even the vastly expensive navy fulfilled expectations. Several cruisers were lost as early as August 1914 and although the German fleet suffered fewer losses than Britain at Jutland in May 1916, by then submarine power was superseding battleships. Tirpitz, the architect of the costly battleship programme, was forced to resign. On the eastern front the Germany army, commanded by Generals Hindenberg and Ludendorff, had greater success in driving Russian troops out of east Prussia as early as the end of August 1914 but this victory was short-lived.

On the home front civilians suffered severely. No plans had been made for a long war. Indeed, some historians have argued that Germany had no plans for a war at all; no preparations had been made to ensure adequate food supplies, resources for the military or labour for industry. As early as 1915 food was in short supply, largely because the British blockade prevented much-needed imports from reaching the German people. Bread rationing was introduced in June 1915 and potatoes were in such limited supply that farmers were forbidden to feed them to their animals. Shortage goods were distributed unevenly and prices were high. The only people who profited from this situation were the black marketeers and, as conditions worsened in the towns, there were food riots, looting of food shops and strikes, often by women and young people. The Kaiser's civil truce was at an end. 1916 saw a worsening of the food situation with the winter of 1916–17 being dubbed the 'turnip winter' because this unappetizing vegetable formed the staple ingredient of people's diets. The supply of bread was inadequate, and many farmers stopped taking their wares to market to prevent them from being snatched out of their hands by desperate women. It is estimated that around 700,000 Germans starved to death on the home front during the war. After the cessation of hostilities a high level of malnutrition was discovered and many young people were pronounced unfit for work. The sense of community spirit which had accompanied the first few months of the war gave way to a heightened awareness of social inequality. The poor were indignant and angry at the profiteers and the rich who hoarded goods, could afford to buy on the black market and were not fighting at the front.

Food shortages were accompanied by a munitions crisis. All stocks of ammunition had been used up by October 1914, and because so many industrial workers had been sent to the front (by 1918 almost half of all German men between the ages of 15 and 60 had been called up) factories were short of labour power (particularly skilled labour), a situation partially alleviated by the employment of women in the war industries. By 1918 there were 2.3 million women employed in industry compared with 1.6 million in 1913. Wages for munitions workers were somewhat better than those paid in non-war industries, particularly for women, but on the negative side working conditions were worse as hours increased and welfare protection laws were lifted for the war's duration. Workers who were not getting enough to eat suffered from illness and fatigue and were more likely to suffer an accident at work. In contrast, the entrepreneurs profited from the war, leading to more resentment amongst the workers. In April 1917 there were strikes across Germany and again, on a larger scale, in January and February 1918. Class differences were intensified rather than alleviated by the war.

The combination of unrest at home and setbacks in the military campaign, an argument about submarine warfare and the entry of the United States into the war in April 1917, precipitated the resignation of Bethmann Hollweg and his replacement with a military government led by Generals Hindenburg and Ludendorff in July 1917. Despite evidence suggesting the war was not progressing as satisfactorily as they might have hoped, some Germans of right-wing tendencies advocated annexation of areas in eastern and western Europe and measures to punish the enemy for their assault on Germany. In contrast, on the far left there were calls for peace. After 1916 it was no longer possible to claim that Germany was defending herself against autocratic Russia. The leading Spartacist, Karl Liebknecht, addressed thousands on 1 May 1916 calling for peace and revolution. He was promptly arrested but a wave of sympathy strikes indicated that his call had tapped a widespread sentiment amongst the working class. Undoubtedly the Russian revolution of 1917 had an impact on the German people and the strikes at the beginning of 1918 in which a million workers participated, were politically motivated. Despite the essential contribution of the working class to the war effort there had been no political reform.

By 1918, when it was clear the war was lost, war-weariness was manifested in anger against the authorities. Throughout the war years the working class had become increasingly radical as a result of the deterioration of conditions and the absence of any political change. There was a total lack of confidence in the civilian authorities and at times it seemed as if no-one was in control. As a consequence of war-weariness, longing for peace but above all, anger and resentment at the ruling classes, German workers joined in the revolutionary unrest in November 1918.

Revolution

At the beginning of October 1918 the military leaders handed power to a civilian government led by a new chancellor, Prince Max von Baden. The purpose was both to pre-empt a harsh peace treaty imposed by the Allies and to head off further domestic unrest. In what has been called a 'revolution from above', fundamental parliamentary reforms were introduced including ministerial responsibility to parliament, civilian control of the armed forces and abolition of the Prussian three-class voting system. However, Wilhelm II refused to abdicate, despite popular pressure for him to do so.

Few were contented with these limited constitutional changes and during the armistice negotiations in October 1918, the Chief of the Admiralty ordered the German fleet to sail out of Wilhelmshaven to carry out what would have been a suicidal attack on the British. Realizing this, a majority of the sailors refused orders. The sailors' mutiny was the first act in a revolutionary wave that swept across Germany in November 1918. Councils of sailors, soldiers and workers were established on the Bolshevik model, from Hamburg in the north down to southern Bavaria, where a socialist government was set up under Kurt Eisner. The government in Berlin had lost control.

Max von Baden resigned on 9 November, handing over power to the SPD leader Friedrich Ebert. In the afternoon of that day the Social Democrat Philipp Scheidemann spontaneously announced, 'The Hohenzollerns have abdicated. Long live the great German Republic', and in the evening Wilhelm fled over the border to Holland.

Scheidemann's rather precipitate proclamation did nothing to subdue the unrest in the country. Although officially Germany had a socialist government, power was still challenged by the radical workers' and soldiers' council movement and some wished to see more fundamental change. Among these were the Independent Social Democrats in the government, who eventually left the cabinet in December 1918 in protest at Ebert's moderate policy, and the Spartacists, founded by Karl Liebknecht and Rosa Luxemburg, who were disillusioned with German Social Democracy in its guise as a bureaucratic party organization bereft of ideas and out of touch with the masses.

Of course Ebert was faced with massive problems: the armistice, the demobilization of returning soldiers, ensuring food supplies and constructing a new constitution in the face of continuing revolutionary upheaval. Ebert chose to compromise with the elites at the expense of a thoroughgoing transformation of the German political and economic system. First of all, Ebert came to an agreement with General Groener, head of the Supreme Command. If Ebert would adopt a moderate course and suppress radicalism Groener guaranteed the support of the army for the new regime. Ebert complied, and when in the first few months of 1919 it looked as if the government was under serious threat from Spartacist uprisings, Ebert used the Free Corps – volunteer militia forces raised by former imperial officers – to brutally suppress the unrest. In the process they murdered Liebknecht and Luxemburg. Ebert's second compromise was with the industrialists. An agreement between the trade union leader Carl Legien and Hugo Stinnes, the industrialist, appeared to guarantee improved labour conditions including the eight-hour day. It was not long, however, in the severe economic circumstances of the new regime, before the industrialists reneged on the agreement. The criticism of Ebert, then, is that he put the securing of order above radical political change.

In January 1919 elections were held to elect a National Assembly. The Constituent Assembly met on 6 February in

65

Weimar since the imperial capital, Berlin, was considered too exposed to the threat of revolutionary violence. The SPD won only 38 per cent of the vote and thus had to form a coalition government with the Catholic Centre Party and the liberal German Democratic Party. Ebert was elected President on 11 February 1919.

Thus, Germany had a new regime known as the Weimar Republic. The new constitution was progressive in that it incorporated proportional representation, an elected president, universal suffrage, and a cabinet responsible to parliament. But with the new constitution the Republic's problems were only just starting. The Versailles Peace Settlement imposed very harsh terms on Germany, the Republic continued to face threats from the right and left until 1923, and perhaps the most destabilizing problem of all, the economy plunged into a state of crisis. This is not the place to discuss the problems of the Weimar Republic but it is interesting to note that some elements of the old Wilhelmine regime survived, ultimately to challenge the regime's legitimacy in 1933.

Conclusions

The social tensions which had festered and rumbled under the surface of the Wilhelmine regime rose to the surface in 1918 after four years of war which had intensified class conflict and revealed the ruling elite as a conservative, unrepresentative oligarchy. The war had demonstrated that an industrially mature nation which perpetuated an immature political system could not hope to survive without a challenge to its legitimacy. The 'politics of notables' was thoroughly tested during the war and found wanting. The war had produced a social and political crisis prompting a desire for change, not just amongst the working class but within broad sections of the middle class too. Between 1914 and 1918 the structural weaknesses of the Empire, which had originated in the Bismarckian era and been perpetuated under Wilhelm II, had been fatally revealed.

6

Continuities and discontinuities
in German history

The 1990s are a good time to reconsider the course of German history after the reunification of a divided nation. Much has been made in this Pamphlet of the paradox of the German Empire: the incongruity of a modernizing industrial economy overlaid by an authoritarian, semi absolutist state. This was Germany's so called peculiarity. It has been argued that because she failed to modernize her political structure, denying the new social classes effective political representation and incorporating the bourgeoisie into the state, Germany travelled a different path from her western European neighbours, a *Sonderweg*, which ultimately led to the catastrophe of the Third Reich.

This continuity theory of German history, argued from the foreign policy perspective by Fritz Fischer in his controversial book *Germany's Aims in the First World War*, and more recently from the perspective of the primacy of domestic policy by Hans Ulrich Wehler in *The German Empire 1871–1918*, has been questioned in recent years, particularly by social historians who have emphasized the lives of ordinary people as much as the actions of the political elites. This Pamphlet has tried to keep in sight the interpretations of the continuity advocates as well as their critics. It has attempted to combine the approaches of 'history from above' and 'history from below'. It has tried to maintain a balance between the practice of politics and diplomacy by the ruling elites, and the forces of economic and social change experienced by ordinary Germans. And whilst recognizing the key role of Bismarck, and to a lesser extent Wilhelm II, in the formation and implementation of domestic and foreign policy, the pressures from below, from Protestants and Catholics, workers, women, peasants and pressure groups, have been accorded attention since the German Empire was not a uniform political entity subject to manipulation on a grand scale.

While there is little doubt that Bismarck adopted repressive and manipulative tactics in order to preserve the status quo, there is a question mark over the effectiveness of these strategies. Repressed groups like Catholics and socialists had a tendency to bounce back, the indoctrination of the German people was only ever partially successful, and the lower classes were not pacified by social reform or colonial adventures. After 1890, with Bismarck gone, there was a groundswell of political activity which mounted a challenge to elite dominance of public and political life. Workers, women, peasants and the middle classes increasingly articulated their grievances via pressure groups while the political parties became enmeshed in an ineffective series of coalitions. Far from the elites manipulating the masses with their programme of foreign aggression and military expansion, the masses exerted pressure on the political system. The outbreak of the First World War permitted the elites temporarily to retain their grip on power. However, after the dislocations and tensions of war the pre-war challenges rose to the surface once more, but now in a direct confrontation with a discredited state and an out-of-touch Kaiser.

Bismarck and Wilhelm II were undoubtedly central actors in the creation, consolidation and eventual unravelling of the German Empire but ordinary German people were more than mere puppets. A complete understanding of Germany between unification and revolution depends on an analysis of the interaction between the rulers and the ruled. Just as in 1989 when the collapse of the Communist regime in east Germany resulted from mass demonstrations by ordinary citizens as well as the actions of leading politicians, so in 1918–19 the collapse of the German Empire was a product of a people's uprising and political and military mismanagement. The German Empire was not merely a stage on the road to the National Socialist Third

Reich; but the failure to accommodate the Empire's diverse constituency did store up problems for the future which the Nazis were able to exploit.

The recent unification of east and west Germany has prompted historians once again to reassess the 'German question'. Germany is once again a unitary nation state in the heart of a Europe characterized by the revival of nationalism. And once again, as during the Second Empire of Bismarck and Wilhelm II, Germany is struggling to consolidate herself in political, economic and social terms. The so-called 'German problem' has not completely disappeared. The attempts to integrate the planned communist economy of the five eastern states into the advanced capitalist economy of the Federal Republic is producing severe social dislocation. In the east rising unemployment has resulted in severe deprivation and has fuelled resentment against foreigners. In the west there is some unease at the financial cost of unification. The extremely rapid process of political and economic unification – less than a year separated the fall of the Berlin Wall from official unification – has highlighted the considerable social and cultural differences between inhabitants of the former east and west (*Ossis* and *Wessis*) which derived from two very different political cultures which developed between 1945 and 1989.

However, despite these structural problems, we should not fall into the trap of ascribing to the new nation state the characteristics or the problems of its Bismarckian predecessor. The German nation state of today is a democratic, federal state, firmly integrated into the European Union. Many Germans express allegiance to Europe before identification with the nation, a legacy of the extreme nationalism propagated by the Third Reich. Early fears by some outside Germany regarding the economic strength of a unified Germany in the centre of Europe have been partially assuaged in the light of economic problems arising from restructuring. And finally, if another argument were needed to quash the assertions of those who emphasize continuity, we might question the whole idea of a unitary German nation state. Bismarck's Germany was an artificial creation which only survived until 1919 in its original geographical and political sense. Hitler destroyed the vestiges of this state, and in 1949 Germany was partitioned. The new German nation state may be seen just as another recasting of Germany's boundaries. Although historical preoccupation with continuity in German history has provided a great many insights, now may be the time to reject any notion of an essential German nation state and accept that the idea of Germany has always been flexible and subject to change and interpretation.

Notes

1 Quoted in H.-U. Wehler, *The German Empire, 1871–1918*, Leamington Spa, 1985, p. 232.
2 D. Geary, *Hitler and Nazism*, London, 1993.
3 This argument has been put forward strongly by Wehler in *The German Empire*.
4 Quoted in R. J. Evans, 'Wilhelm II's Germany and the historians', in R. J. Evans (ed.), *Rethinking German History*, London, 1987, p. 45.
5 For example, the essays in R. J. Evans (ed.), *Society and Politics in Wilhelmine Germany*, London, 1978, and R. J. Evans (ed.), *The German Working Class, 1888–1933*, London, 1982.
6 For a negative assessment of Bismarck see E. Crankshaw, *Bismarck*, London, 1981; a more measured analysis is L. Gall's *Bismarck: The White Revolutionary*, London, 1987.
7 I. V. Hull, *The Entourage of Kaiser Wilhelm II 1888–1918*, Cambridge, 1982, p. 304.
8 J. Röhl and N. Sombart (eds), *Kaiser Wilhelm II: New Interpretations*, Cambridge, 1982, credits Wilhelm II with considerable influence.
9 Gall, *Bismarck*, p. 343.
10 Helmut Böhme quoted in G. Eley, 'Bismarckian Germany', in G. Martel (ed.), *Modern Germany Reconsidered, 1870–1945*, London, 1992, p. 12.

11 See D. Blackbourn and G. Eley, *The Peculiarities of German History*, Oxford, 1985, and D. Blackbourn and R. J. Evans (eds), *The German Bourgeoisie*, London, 1991.
12 Quoted in G. Craig, *Germany 1866–1945*, Oxford, 1981, p.179.
13 See D. Blackbourn, *Populists and Patricians*, London, 1987, p. 222.
14 R. Henig, *The Origins of the First World War*, London, 1989, 2nd edition 1993.
15 F. Fischer, *Germany's Aims in the First World War*, London, 1961; Wehler, *The German Empire*.

Further reading

The following is a selection of further reading available in the English language.

There are a number of good surveys of modern German history available which include accounts of the imperial period. The best are William A. Carr, *A History of Germany 1815–1990* (4th edition, London, 1991); Gordon A. Craig, *Germany, 1866–1945* (4th edition, Oxford, 1992); Hajo Holborn, *A History of Modern Germany 1840–1945* (Princeton, 1969). From a social historical standpoint there is Eda Sagarra, *A Social History of Germany 1648–1914* (London, 1977). For a much broader survey see Mary Fulbrook, *A Concise History of Germany* (Cambridge, 1990).

Still the most stimulating if controversial recent interpretation of the German Empire is Hans-Ulrich Wehler's *The German Empire 1871–1918* (Leamington Spa, 1985). Wehler's provocative viewpoint has prompted considerable debate. The collection of essays edited by Richard J. Evans, *Society and Politics in Wilhelmine Germany* (London, 1978) is critical of Wehler and suggests some new interpretations. Gordon Martel (ed.), *Modern Germany Reconsidered, 1870–1945* (London, 1992) contains useful essays summing up the present state of research in this field. On the question of the German *Sonderweg* and Germany's alleged peculiar development a good starting point is Geoff Eley and David Blackbourn, *The Peculiarities of*

German History: Bourgeois Society and Politics in Nineteenth Century Germany (Oxford, 1984). The industrial revolution is considered in W. O. Henderson, *The Rise of German Industrial Power, 1834–1914* (London, 1975), and the effects of urbanization are dramatically portrayed in Richard J. Evans, *Death in Hamburg: Society and Politics in the Cholera Years* (Oxford, 1987).

Bismarck has been the subject of numerous biographies. The best include A. J. P. Taylor's *Bismarck: The Man and Statesman* (London, 1955) and Lothar Gall's more recent *Bismarck: The White Revolutionary* (London, 1980). Wilhelm II has similarly attracted historians' attention; see John Röhl, *Germany without Bismarck* (Stanford, 1967); John Röhl and Nicolaus Sombart (eds), *Kaiser Wilhelm II: New Interpretations* (Cambridge, 1982); and Thomas A. Kohut, *Wilhelm II and the Germans: A Study in Leadership* (Oxford, 1991).

The unification of Germany is discussed in almost any general text but for more detailed examination see Theodor Hamerow, *The Social Foundations of German Unification 1858–1871* (Princeton, 1968), W. Carr, *The Wars of German Unification* (London, 1991), Otto Pflanze, *Bismarck and the Development of Germany: The Period of Unification 1815–1871* (Princeton, 1990) and a briefer study using primary documents by David Hargreaves, *Bismarck and German Unification* (London, 1991). On the question of German identity and nationalism see Harold James, *A German Identity 1770–1990* (London, 1989), Michael Hughes, *Nationalism and Society: Germany 1800–1945* (London, 1988) and John Breuilly (ed.), *The State of Germany* (London, 1992).

German society in this period has received belated attention in recent years. Amongst numerous studies of the working class and the Social Democratic Party some of the most useful include: Richard J. Evans (ed.), *The German Working Class 1888–1945: The Politics of Everyday Life* (London, 1982); Stephen H. F. Hickey, *Workers in Imperial Germany: The Miners of the Ruhr* (Oxford, 1985); W. L. Guttsman, *The German Social Democratic Party 1875–1933* (London, 1981). Catholics and the Centre Party are well documented in David Blackbourn, *Class, Religion and Local Politics in Wilhelmine Germany* (Yale, 1980) and Jonathon Sperber, *Popular Catholicism in Nineteenth Century Germany* (Princeton, 1984). Ute

Frevert's *Women in German History* (Leamington Spa, 1989) is the best general survey of women in modern Germany while the feminist movement is charted by Richard J. Evans in *The Feminist Movement in Germany 1894–1933* (London, 1976). For information on the peasantry see Richard J. Evans and W. R. Lee (eds), *The German Peasantry* (London, 1986).

The position of the ruling elites in Germany is well documented. On the Conservative Party there is James Retallack's *Notables of the Right: The Conservative Party and Political Mobilization in Germany, 1876–1918* (London, 1988). On other right-wing political groupings see Geoff Eley, *Reshaping the Right: Radical Nationalism and Political Change after Bismarck* (Yale, 1980). The officer corps has been documented by Martin Kitchen in *The German Officer Corps* (London, 1968), and on the Pan-German League see Roger Chickering, *We Men Who Feel Most German: A Cultural Study of the Pan-German League* (Boston, Mass., 1984).

Finally, the foreign policies of Bismarck and Wilhelm II have been treated exhaustively. The classic study is Fritz Fischer's *Germany's Aims in the First World War* (London, 1961). In support of the Fischer thesis see Volker Berghahn, *Germany and the Approach of War in 1914* (London, 1973). See also Paul Kennedy, *The Rise of the Anglo-German Antagonism, 1860–1914* (London, 1980). On imperial policy Hans-Ulrich Wehler's 'Bismarck's imperialism 1862–1890' in *Past and Present*, vol. 48 (1970) summarizes his arguments. The experience of the First World War on the home front is discussed by Jurgen Kocka in *Facing Total War: German Society 1914–1918* (Leamington Spa, 1984), and for the experience of trench warfare see Modris Eksteins, *Rites of Spring: The Great War and the Birth of the Modern Age* (London, 1989). On the revolution of 1918–19 see A. J. Ryder, *The German Revolution* (Cambridge, 1967).

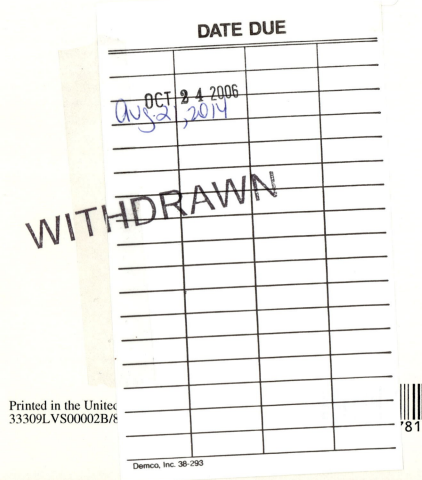

DATE DUE

OCT 2 4 2006

WITHDRAWN

Printed in the Unite
33309LVS00002B/8

'811

Demco, Inc. 38-293